PRAISE FOR *COMPETITIVE SELLING*
AND THE AUTHORS

"Cold calling is not dead! If your business needs a steady stream of new prospects to survive (and frankly who doesn't), then this book will provide you with the tools, strategies, and common sense inspiration to make those calls and close those sales. Stacia and Marisa break down the exact map you need to implement what they call competitive selling, so you can get over that fear and frustration of cold calling and start pushing your business or your sales career to the next level. Read it now!"

SUE KIRCHNER, PRESIDENT
BRAND STRONG MARKETING, INC.

"Finally, a training partner that actually rolls up their sleeves and helps your organization increase SALES!

"For more than a decade, Marisa Pensa and Methods in Motion have been trusted business advisors and key resources for my growing business. Her "no-nonsense" approach and process-driven selling methodology is practical, powerful and proven. In the crowded space of sales training organizations, Marisa stands out as one of very few trainers who is actually willing to both provide the road map and then ride shotgun with you!

"Read this book, apply these lessons, do the hard work, stick with it, and watch it grow!"

BRIAN D. ROSSI, SERIAL ENTREPRENEUR AND REAL ESTATE INVESTOR
CEO, STARPINE PROPERTIES, LLC AND BDR & ASSOCIATES, INC.
PARTNER, SUNBELT OFFICE PRODUCTS

"Anyone in sales looking to help others meet their goals will value the concrete advice in *Competitive Selling*. From knowing who to target to providing clear, succinct messaging, the approaches found in this book truly help you stand out amongst your competition. This guidebook provides easy-to-apply techniques, whether on the phone or in the field, to engage prospects and get results."

**KEVIN HIMMEL, VICE PRESIDENT OF OPERATIONS
THE REGIS COMPANY**

"If you are in business today and just reacting to what's happening around you, you probably won't be in business very long. Being proactive and competitive in your selling approach is key to success, but fundamentally you must also continue to bring value to your clients and customers.

"Marisa Pensa and Stacia Skinner have put together the definitive book on proactive calling you won't want to miss having in your business library and you'll also want to make it required reading for each member of your sales team."

**STACY A. BELL, DIRECTOR, SALES OPERATIONS
S.P. RICHARDS COMPANY**

"With the accelerating pace at which buying and selling is evolving, the winning sellers are those who are constantly learning and adjusting. Stacia and Marisa have masterfully distilled these new complexities into an easily digestible, fun and actionable resource filled with indispensable concepts to master prospecting."

**TODD CAPONI
AUTHOR OF *THE TRANSPARENCY SALE***

"Sales is challenging, however after reading this book, you will have the tools to WIN in the highly competitive sales world. This book provides the real fundamentals for successful selling."

ROLAND "ROLLY" DYCK, BUSINESS RESOURCE COACH
SOPE

"If you think picking up the phone is not the way to gain new customers, then you need to read this book. We can all fall into the habit of being reactive and waiting for our phone to ring or hoping someone will answer our email. But how is this giving you the competitive edge? This book will provide you what you need. Stacia and Marisa have put together a step-by-step guideline that will walk you through how to get past the distractions your customers encounter every day in order to win against your competition!"

JEFFREY A. NIESEN, SENIOR VICE PRESIDENT
BANKER'S BANK

"*Competitive Selling* gives you the essential information you need to differentiate yourself from your competitors in the consultative sales process. This book provides a great blueprint for improving your sales skills by being proactive and intentional."

SKIP MANCINI, PRESIDENT
B.T. MANCINI

"The sales profession experiences seismic changes from time to time. In this book, Stacia Skinner and Marisa Pensa capture the essence of must-have, interruptive, outcome-based selling skills essential to remaining relevant and successful in our profession.

"Sales will always be a competitive sport. It is no longer sufficient to have a well-prepared pitch—the sales professionals that understand how a customer does business and brings value to the discussion—wins."

NELLIE SCOTT, CHANNEL DEVELOPMENT MANAGER, GLOBAL ALLIANCES & CHANNELS SAS INSTITUTE INC.

"Methods In Motion is a professional and disciplined company that is concerned about making it right for their clients. With the success of their customers in mind, this book was written providing the tools to achieve sales goals."

**TODD PALCIT, CO-OWNER
MONARCH BASICS**

"Stacia and Marisa are top professionals who do the two things only the best trainers do: the first is to actually close sales and build a successful business following their own advice. The second is to actually grow their client's sales and do so year over year. Their oldest clients and their constantly growing client lists are proof of both of those things. They offer strategies and tactics and the professional development steps needed to be a top salesperson in any industry."

**STEVE BOOKBINDER, CEO
DIGITAL MEDIA TRAINING, INC.
AUTHOR OF *HOW TO BE YOUR OWN COACH, NETWORKING TO WIN,*
AND *LEVERAGE YOUR LAZINESS***

"Stacia has worked with our field sales force for years, stressing not only the importance of prospecting but how to reach the decision maker with an impactful approach. Many people say sales people are born, not made. I beg to differ as I've seen Stacia give them the tools to succeed time after time. Stacia will always be my favorite 'Tuesday at 2' appointment."

KEVIN KELLY, VICE PRESIDENT, SALES
HYATT PLACE & HYATT HOUSE

"I can attest to this day that Stacia's expertise in a proactive and competitive selling approach, building one's brand and business etiquette have greatly improved my sales success. She continues to offer great coaching and is extremely approachable. I consistently utilize Stacia's sales tips and advice on a daily basis. Stacia's book is a testament to her wealth of knowledge in helping others become successful in their field."

CASEY S. BERMAN, SENIOR REGIONAL EXECUTIVE DIRECTOR
ACADEMIC PARTNERSHIPS

"In spite of the effect that the internet has had on how many people shop, the telephone still remains the best tool for reaching out to truly connect with customers and develop customer loyalty. From the initial cold call to following up once the order is placed, there is a roadmap to effective selling and this book will help you find that path. Marisa Pensa has personally helped our telephone sales team grow in confidence, ability and most of all results for several years now. Her understanding of the ecosystem that is phone sales is extraordinary."

MATT ROBISON, DIRECTOR OF SALES
AIRGAS, AN AIR LIQUIDE COMPANY

COMPETITIVE SELLING

COMPETITIVE
SELLING

THE GUIDEBOOK TO PROACTIVE CALLING
IN A REACTIVE WORLD

Takeem :
May you always have an appointment
Tuesday @ 3:00
~ Stacia ~

STACIA
SKINNER

MARISA
PENSA

BIG DOGS
PUBLISHING

Published by Big Dogs Publishing

Cover and Interior Design by Imagine! Studios
www.ArtsImagine.com

Cover Photo: iStock.com/Sean_Gao

ISBN: 978-1-7338531-0-1 (paperback)
ISBN: 978-1-7338531-1-8 (e-book)

Library of Congress Control Number: 2019904286

First Big Dogs Publishing printing: April 2019

TABLE OF CONTENTS

PREFACE AND ACKNOWLEDGMENTS

Let's start by answering the question: Why did we decide to write this book in the first place? Being in the training industry (Stacia with over twenty-two years in the business and Marisa with over fifteen years), we were frustrated with what was out there for helping salespeople do their jobs better. Either the books were old school and talked about the "world wide web" for goodness sakes (are you kidding?), or they just didn't provide a simple way to achieve appointments. They overcomplicated everything so you didn't even know how to say "Hello"! As a result, we decided to put our own skills together and come up with the Competitive Selling concept as a guidebook for outbound calling.

Every book talks about being consultative and listening to the customer, and we get that! However, to really win at this sales game you have to be better, smarter, and sometimes go back and relook at what you already know and tweak it a bit to get a different result. That is what we are providing in this book: practical, easy, and pragmatic ways to gain that all-important first appointment or initial phone conversation. It does not matter what industry you are in. You have to start somewhere. Without that very first engagement with a potential customer, you got DIRT!

When we do our training programs and ask the question: "How many of you like to cold call?" it is a rarity that we get the room exploding with hands raised and people shouting, "I do, I do, I do!" Instead we get crickets chirping and everyone looking around the room to see who is going to brown-nose the instructor today!

We have to step outside of our comfort zone to talk to people we don't know! But that's the necessary evil we have to do as salespeople in order to grow our business, gain that commission check, prepare for natural attrition, or achieve the President's Club! Let us show you how it is done and share with you what we do each and every day to grow our own businesses. It is proven and it works!!

We would be remiss if we did not thank a few people for helping us get this off the ground. Without their support, love, and cold noses (you will see why!) this would not have happened. First, a thank you from us both to Julie Fabrizius, our in-house wordsmith who did an incredible job helping us get our ideas on paper. Also, to Amy Hamilton for the many things she did along the way to help us promote the upcoming of the book and for providing our brand! And to Joe Eckstein and the *I Am Published!* crew, who kept us on target to get the book out in a reasonable amount of time.

From Stacia: I would like to dedicate this book to my Dad. He was my rock and my advisor from the very beginning when I started this business. Thank you, Daddy! And to my husband, Steven Skinner, for putting up with me, supporting me, and being my best critic at hand. Thank you to my kids, Brendan and Colin Skinner, for keeping me grounded and not going absolutely crazy. Thank you to my Mom, who was so excited about this adventure and supported me every step of the way. And last but very not least, thank you to my fur babies, Nala and Jasmine, whose cute little faces put everything back into perspective!

From Marisa: Thank you to my husband, Troy Pensa, for his advice, discernment, and daily sense of humor! Thank you to my precious friend and prayer partner, Carol Williamson, for the prayer that went into this book for hitting deadlines, tapping into creativity, and helping me stay motivated to keep going! And last but not least, thank you to the cold noses in my life, Katie and Maggie.

INTRODUCTION

Competitive selling starts with a proactive outbound call. Let's look at three examples:

- *Stacia's win: "One outbound call to the VP of sales of a major hotel chain resulted in gaining a steady customer, including international business, for the last twelve years."*

- *Marisa's win: "One outbound call to the vice president of a worldwide industrial supplier resulted in conducting inside sales programs for all new hires across call centers in five different cities over the past nine years."*

- *Stacia's win: "One purely cold call to the president of a local multistate bank resulted in a million-dollar account."*

Each of these wins started with picking up the phone, practicing interruptive marketing, and speaking with someone at the right level who had not called us. Outbound prospecting does work. It worked yesterday, it works today, and it will continue to work in the future for those who put in the effort!

Our focus for *Competitive Selling* is to zero in on the very first step in the sales process: *engaging* new prospects, in large enough numbers, on a consistent enough basis to achieve your goals.

Before we dive into the what to do, how to do it, and why to do it at all of prospecting, we want to share this important thought: **We believe sales should never be based on what we are trying to sell, but always be based on how we can help others achieve what they're trying to accomplish.**

This is the difference between pitch selling and consultative selling. But what we want to talk about is *competitive selling*, which is focused on *performance under pressure*. We must sharpen our skills and get even better at what we are already good at. We're playing the game of competitive selling against contenders who are trying to beat us. This is the kind of selling where we take on the role of a trusted advisor. Whenever we initiate a new relationship with an organization, what we're doing is trying to *help* that organization, not *sell* to that organization. That's the driving force behind our interactions with everyone we talk to, every single time.

Stop selling without enhancing the value. Start helping. If you can master this concept, and we know you can, we are absolutely certain you will have no problem adapting to the skills and practices spelled out in *Competitive Selling* to gain the competitive edge and set that all-important first appointment.

Every organization has some type of pipeline to show what's coming up in the future. However, what most salespeople don't master is controlling the front end of the sales process, which is gaining initial appointments in order to engage in conversations. Without a consistent flow of new appointments, it doesn't matter what your pipeline looks like today—at some point it will dry up. Don't allow your pipeline to become a desert, but have a consistent flow, which is something you can control. Achieving this means less stress, fewer headaches, and a better selling atmosphere.

Let's take a moment to consider the last part of the title of this book. What does it mean to live in a "reactive world"? In today's business environment many buyers are complacent or have too many distractions at all times. With email, LinkedIn, Facebook, Twitter, Snapchat, etc., communication is prolific but not always productive. They are constantly reacting to the onslaught of information.

Potential customers also have far more options when it comes to finding out about, researching, and purchasing products and services that in the past they might have needed a salesperson for. People want cheaper, better, and faster. We need to work harder and more *proactively* to shake up the reactive world and help them see the value of what we have to offer. Even if they do not have an immediate need, they could need us in the future.

The goal of *Competitive Selling* is to provide an arsenal of strategies for keeping that steady flow of new business. Whether you work in inside sales or outside sales, contact existing customers for growth, or manage a sales team, our prospecting system provides a step-by-step roadmap for engaging prospects who are not calling you and proactively and creatively starting new conversations each day.

As they say, "Amateurs wing it . . . professionals plan it." None of us can afford to wing this very first call. It can be sales suicide. Having a plan, executing that plan, and measuring the results is the single biggest difference between unproductive and highly successful businesses.

A plan is like a map. When following a plan, you can always see how much you have progressed towards your destination and how far you are from it. Knowing where you are is essential in making good decisions about where to go and what to do next.

Success does not come easily! Yes, some people win the lottery; but that's just by chance. In business, if you rely on chance you can wait a very long time to succeed. In order to get something you really want, you have to work for it. Whether it's getting the lead in a play, being first chair in an orchestra, running a marathon, or gaining that all-important client . . . these things don't happen by chance. They are accomplished with hard work.

In many cases you are faced with doing things you really don't like to do or wish you could avoid. In sales there are two things that sales professionals don't like: being held accountable and driving new business on a consistent basis. Consider sales professionals who always make their goals or exceed their quotas. What do they do that others don't? They hold themselves accountable and have the drive to look for new business. They know they cannot rest on their laurels. They are always looking for ways to bring in more business. They make sure their pipelines have enough in them for sales to come in consistently.

If you are a sales professional, your management team or executive team never tells you, "You had such a great [quarter, month, year] that instead of increasing your [goal, quota, budget] we are going to decrease it since we know you have a lot to do with what you brought in." Instead they say, "Thank you so much for the great [quarter, month, year]. Because you did such a great job we're going to increase your [goal, quota, budget] by ten percent"! We are always relied upon to do more.

This is competitive selling. It's being the best at what you do. We want you to become a competitive seller, especially when it comes to gaining that first appointment. Selling is not just about being consultative. Selling is about being competitive and being better at the game than your competition.

Everyone is a consultative seller. All of us know how to gain new customers, hunt for leads, gain information needed for the sale, present our story, and follow through.

A competitive seller knows how to do all the above; however, they do it at a higher level that exceeds the competition! They get to the new customer before the competition, and they gain information at a deeper level to find out how they can help their customers. They out-present the competition because they show the true impact or value of their products or services in helping that customer. And they develop an environment in which gaining a "next set time" (NST, which we will discuss later) is inevitable.

As we mentioned above, the competitive seller focuses on performing at their very best under pressure. They know the words to say, how to manage their time to get the maximum out of it, and how to track to make sure they exceed their goals.

Just like a professional athlete, musician, or artist, you need the drive, determination, skill, and competitive instinct to be the best at your game. As a professional salesperson, you can't just go out there and expect to be the best; you need a game plan and the skills and determination to be better than the other salespeople who are trying to win the same game. Competitive sellers are the elite athletes who have that little bit of "extra" to be Olympic champions!

We are going to help you get started by providing you with the skills of *proactive calling*. We are going to take you to the next level of making those initial calls to gain the initial appointment, which provides the *edge*, whether on the phone or in the field against your competition. Let's get started.

CHAPTER 1

WHY THE HECK SHOULD I PROSPECT?

Marisa's story: "After reaping the benefits of having a great account for seven long years, an acquisition took place and completely changed everything overnight. There was a new president, and my contacts completely changed, along with their training outlook, which did not include my company. This was devastating to my business. I learned a huge lesson. We've all been there; we put all our eggs in one basket and all of a sudden the basket falls apart."

Think of your number-one customer right now. What would you do if they stopped doing business with you overnight through no fault of your own? Are you thinking this cannot happen? Because it happens more times than not. When you are always prospecting, this situation won't devastate your pocketbook. Neither will attrition. You will enjoy continual growth and won't have to worry about these situations.

We all want to be high-performing salespeople; to achieve goal-crushing sales growth; to be recipients of congratulatory high fives, incentive trips, prizes—and yes, lucrative commission checks. It feels great to win due not to luck but because you and your team worked your tails off to have a lucrative pipeline by following a prospecting routine.

There is a theory stating that sales is divided into thirds. There is a third of contacts who will say yes. There is a third who will say no. And there is a third who could go either way that we call the undecided third.

Luck does play a part sometimes. We call that the first third of the sales pie, or the "yes" category. It's those sales you capture because you're at the right place at the right time. You called and they said, "You know, we were actually considering changing" or "This might be a good time to evaluate vendors." It's music to your ears.

But then there are other contacts who keep telling you they may be interested and to keep following up—even after your twelfth attempt—but they have no intention of buying from you. This third of the pie is the "no" category. No matter what you do they are not going to do business with you. The reason is because they are happy with the competition and are not looking to change. But you can't ask your prospects, "Are you in the 'yes' third or the 'no' third?" You must still treat everyone like potential customers.

The last third of the pie is the undecided category. This is the coveted one-third of sales that you have to fight and claw for. No, you didn't catch them at a good time. They could be happy with what they have now and they could be comfortable where they are. The status quo is your number-one competitor. Proactivity and prospecting are critical in fighting the status quo. This undecided third will determine whether or not you hit or exceed your numbers. This is our area of concentration because this is the area you can control.

This is why we prospect!

Prospects in the undecided third are the cream of the crop among opportunities. It takes a salesperson with a competitive edge to win them. Cream-of-the-crop athletes have this edge and therefore run on rainy days, run when they don't feel like running, and create the muscle-memory to do exactly what they're supposed to do even when they're tired, drained, hungry, or grouchy. Day after day, week after week, month after month, discipline gives them the edge. And that's what you want. You want to be a high-performing, goal-crushing sales pro. Consistently. And not just for the commission check, though that is certainly a motivation. You want it because it shows that you leave everything on the field and that pride in your work matters to you. But what you'll have to bring to the game is the pig-headed discipline, willpower, and stick-to-it-iveness to fill up your coffee mug, put a "Do not disturb" sign on your door or cube, prepare your list, and consistently bang out prospecting calls. Even when it's raining. Even when you don't feel like it.

When working with the undecided third, you have to know how to sell! From the very first call to the closing of the sale. It takes hard work, tenacity, and the will to get the deal. This is where the competitive seller makes the difference. You cannot be consultative; you have to gain the edge and do the right things under pressure to beat your competition. This is how you win sales in the undecided third.

Muscles have memory, and so does your brain. When you do something often enough you get really good at it. You have to create that habit—no one will do it for you.

Unfortunately most salespeople wear many hats, so high performance doesn't happen every month or quarter. They don't have the luxury of prospecting full time or handing off an account to a service team—they *are* the service team. They're also involved in accounts receivable, quality control, firefighting, and many other responsibilities, sometimes all in a single day. In spite of wearing many hats, how do some consistently exceed their goals? The answer is simple: They have decided to be proactive every day. Super performers know that some action is better than no action. One more call. One more proactive email to a prospect who failed to respond to a voicemail. One more personalized note asking to connect on LinkedIn.

Even after all that effort, the cold, hard truth is that many incredible salespeople who are wired to sell and darn good at it still struggle to hit their numbers. They've proven they can do it—built a nice book of repeatable business—but they just got busy servicing, busy firefighting, busy emailing, busy not being proactive about new business development.

Marisa's story: "As in the story at the beginning of this chapter, I counted on having my number-one account forever. And just like that they were gone. When you prospect when you really have to, you sound desperate. And no one wants to sound desperate."

New business is the lifeblood of any organization. Every year some percentage of customers is not going to come back, even through no fault of your own. Two CEOs play golf together, and just like that the business is lost.

Think again about your number-one customer . . . if you lost them tomorrow, would you have enough in your pipeline to make up that business, or could you make it up in a relatively short time? This is an important question to ask yourself, and a reality check. If you're new to your organization and can't answer that question yet, that's okay. The goal is to get you thinking about always being proactive. Grow new accounts, grow the spend-within-buying accounts, and consistently sell people more stuff that's going to help them.

. . . Easier said than done. As another author put it, "Prospecting sucks. Get over it." It's the truth. Prospecting is the act of interrupting people who didn't call or email you, with the goal of engaging them in a sales conversation. But with the strategies in *Competitive Selling* you can be fantastic at prospecting and create the habit to keep it going.

ACTION STEP

Write down the name of your number-one customer. If their business went away, how long would it take you to replace that business based on your current pipeline?

If you are feeling a bit nervous with your answer, don't fret. Keep reading!

CHAPTER 2

SMOKIN' TOO MUCH HOPIUM

We only prospect as much as we feel we need to.

Stacia's story: "I had a client in the office products industry who had prepared an executive overview of what their department was going to bring in for the quarter. All the salespeople had looked at their pipelines and projected exactly what they thought would close. The sales manager knew some would sandbag and predict that everything in their pipelines would close. The manager thought he had adjusted the forecast to account for overoptimism, but when we really started digging we found that the salespeople had no control over 80 percent of opportunities in their pipelines. The projection went from $4 million to $500,000. The manager, after the training, had to go back to the executive team and tell them there was a huge discrepancy because he realized that the team had been smoking 'hopium.'"

What is hopium, and how do you avoid it? Hopium is counting on and forecasting sales that are out of your control because you don't have a "next set time"(or NST)—a mutually agreed-on date and time on your prospect's calendar when you will talk or meet again to move the sale forward. Rather than relying on a gut feeling, your next set time is evidence that your prospect is playing ball with you. Without an NST you can't rely on that prospect for income.

We've all heard these statements; they give us that glimmer of hope:

- "We'll have a decision by next week."
- "Haven't had time to look at the contract, but I'll get to it any day now."
- "I like what I see and I'll get back to you."

They make us feel like we've accomplished something when in reality we're just hoping and wishing these sales come through. We don't have any concrete evidence that we can count on these opportunities or even that we will meet again with the client.

Hope clouds reality. Hope is not a sales strategy. Be aware of what's really happening with your potential customers so you can fine-tune your approach, ask the right questions, and make appropriate adjustments before it's too late. You don't get paid for wishes and hopes; you get paid for what's real.

When you're overly optimistic about the business you expect to come in, you don't prospect enough. Who wants to prospect if they don't have to? So when the hopium smoke clears and sales for the month look terrible, you get desperate. And because you *are* desperate, you *sound* desperate.

We've all been there. We would rather hear a yes than a no. Unfortunately we are in the business of hearing no. We have to get the no in order to get the yes. Think of it as a "no" quota.

Marisa's story: "I used to have a boss who would ask me weekly, "How many nos did you get this week?" Then he would ask, "How many more nos do you need this week?" It shifted my mindset. I had to hit my 'no' quota weekly. It sounds silly but it worked to put a more positive spin on the nos, since I knew how many I had to get!"

This is why sales is not easy. Ask anyone who is not in sales how they would feel after getting bombarded with the word *no* most of the time. That's why they are not in sales.

When you think you have enough in your pipeline, hopium is high and you lose sight of the front end of your pipeline. You are totally focused on what's closing. Sticking to a regular prospecting routine and staying proactive helps you avoid the ups and downs of sales—in other words, the desperation and chaos!

We have all experienced it—a great May, a terrible June, a great July, a terrible August. This happens because what we think we have versus what we really have are two different things. We don't take into account the ratios we need in order to keep our pipelines full.

Let's say you have a 5:1 closing ratio. You get one hundred leads and twenty prospects from those leads. You go on five sales calls and you close one. How many prospects do you have left? Many will say nineteen, but in reality you have fifteen, because no one has a 1:1 closing ratio. You have a 5:1 closing ratio, so you have fifteen prospects, not nineteen. But you still work as though you have nineteen. You sell one more and you think you have eighteen left, when you really have ten. And you go down the line until you hit zero. All of a sudden it feels like every deal has fallen through. What happened is you didn't refill your pipeline along the way. Now it's too late to do anything about the past. What you can do is learn from this and plan your prospecting routine so it doesn't happen again.

What is your closing ratio? Is it 5:1? 4:1? This determines what you need on the front end of your pipeline. There's a magic number, and it's different for everyone. You should know how much effort it will take to close. Stacia needs to have five or six first appointments scheduled over a two-week period at all times to hit her goal. When she first started in the business she had to have twelve to fourteen first appointments in that two-week period because she was learning. That was her number.

Let's consider where your results come from.

$$A \times E = R$$
Activity × Efficiency = Results

Between activity and efficiency, which one is currently your strength? Only one involves a decision. You can *decide* to be more active (or more proactive), but you can't decide to be more efficient. While activity is a decision, efficiency is learned. If you don't have enough activity but your efficiency is high, you can still miss your goals; you're not setting yourself up to get that "undecided" third of business we referred to earlier.

Driving up your activity can be anything from time-blocking your day or using an old-fashioned tick-sheet to keep yourself brutally honest, to making just three more calls before lunch or making one more call at the end of the day. There has to be a balance between activity and efficiency to get the results you want. That balance is different for everyone, but make sure you have it.

Which brings us to the difference between being proactive and reactive in your daily activity. If you were to examine your level of activity—being proactive versus reactive—where would most of your activity be? If I said: "We have to react to this current situation," what comes to mind? "There is no plan"? "I'm behind the eight ball"? "We're in a losing situation"? The stress level begins to accelerate. It is not a fun place to be, nor is it a productive place to be in sales. In many cases it can be very destructive to the bottom-line.

Here are some reactive activities to be aware of:

- Answering emails to serve customers
- Firefighting
- Servicing existing accounts without upselling or cross-selling
- Handling administrative duties
- Cleaning your office during prime selling hours
- Doing busywork that is not high-impact

When you think about being proactive, what comes to mind? "We have a plan"? "We have a strategy"? "I'm on top of the situation and planning in advance for expected issues or slumps"? How does that feel in comparison?

Here are some proactive activities that can help you:

- Prospecting over the phone (new accounts and growing existing accounts)

- Spending face-to-face time with prospects and customers who are looking for new business
- Strategizing your next call and planning how you will win the business
- Networking, attending new events
- Closing sales!

To help you clear the air of too much hopium, here are some easy things you can do right now to keep these proactive activities in check:

FIRST TIP: *Create the habit of scheduling your time.*

Everything needs a scheduled time. Stacia has a date/time (a next set time) for her next appointment. She has time scheduled to do her proposals. She has time scheduled with her manager. She has time scheduled to prospect. Create the habit of attaching a time element to everything you do. Without it you will not be in control of your day, which also means you will not be in control of your sales.

SECOND TIP: *Have a plan.*

The one with the best plan wins. In today's competitive market you can't afford to just wing the steps of your sales process. If you don't have the best plan, someone behind you will, and you'll lose the deal. Have a plan for what you will say on the phone. Have a planned objective for your meeting. Have a plan to knock down barriers that could get in the way. Have a plan to proactively deal with a prospect's objections. When networking, have a plan to meet three specific people, and don't leave the event until you have accomplished that goal.

THIRD TIP: *Always be closing.*

Those famous words from the screenplay *Glengarry Glen Ross* by David Mamet are still true today: "Always be closing." However, in this context "closing" can be closing on making an appointment, closing on a next set time, or actually closing a sale. Does being reactive ever work when it comes to closing a sale? Sometimes, yes; the customer just comes to us. But most of us can't rely on those easy sales to hit our numbers. We need to proactively guide prospects to the next step and use our skills to ultimately close the sale.

When you snuff out hopium you can face the truth of what's in your pipeline. You can structure your days and be a better forecaster of what business is coming in. Structure without chaos equals more dollars in your pocket. And we can all use more of those!

ACTION STEPS

1. Look at your pipeline and your calendar. Count how many of your prospects have your name in their calendars with a scheduled date and time to speak or meet in the next two weeks.

2. Commit to a number of dials that you will do for the next two weeks and put it on a sticky note on your computer. Follow through and do it!

3. Schedule critical activities. This includes blocking out time on your calendar to prospect, do proposals, and find leads, and keeping to your schedule to make sure you are making time to be proactive.

CHAPTER 3

IDENTIFYING THE KEY PLAYERS AND GETTING YOUR S#%T TOGETHER

To help with the task of calling, there's a very simple organizational chart you can master in a matter of minutes. Once you do, you will find it much easier to put the principles of the *Competitive Selling* prospecting system into action.

Don't worry; this isn't one of those interminable mapping exercises that demands you identify the name and title of every individual in every office of a certain company and draw lines to demonstrate how each one is connected to the rest of the organization. That takes forever, and in our view is unlikely to give you an understanding of your target client.

All we're asking you to do is familiarize yourself with six key people—the six critical players who assume six very different roles as your sale plays out.

PLAYER NUMBER ONE: YOU.

Why start by putting yourself on the organizational chart of your target company? You are, by definition, an agent of positive change. No, you are not an employee of the company; you're something even better. You're the outsider who eventually earns the role of the insider. You're the one who gets all the credit and all the financial rewards of bringing about the kind of change that helps your prospects achieve what they're trying to accomplish. You do that by making the organization more profitable, efficient, and successful.

Understanding your role—the role of an agent of change—is the key to understanding everyone else's role. As you will see, different people react in very different ways to your message of change.

PLAYER NUMBER TWO: HERB.

H.E.R.B. is the Highest Executive Responsible for Buying whatever it is you sell. How can you tell whether or not you're dealing with HERB? It's actually pretty simple. If HERB can, on their own initiative, execute at least 51 percent of the "votes" necessary to determine whether or not something you sell gets purchased, you know you're dealing with HERB. HERB is, in all likelihood, the person who will sign the contract to buy your stuff.

At small organizations, HERB, who has practical control over at least 51 percent of the day-to-day decision-making authority related to buying your stuff, probably has a fancy-sounding title like CEO, chairman, founder, or owner. At large organizations, HERB might have a title like VP of whatever, director of this or that, or chief so-and-so officer. For example, the HERB we typically sell to has the title of VP of sales. But we sell sales training to large enterprises and small businesses, which means we deal with CEOs and founders as well as VPs of sales.

If you're already established with a client and you want to grow the account but you are not working with HERB, we don't recommend leapfrogging over someone you currently have a relationship with to get to HERB. (Growing existing accounts is just as critical as gaining new ones, and we expand on that in later chapters.)

PLAYER NUMBER THREE: THE GRAND POOBAH.

It's easy to see that at large organizations there will be more than one HERB. We refer to the person in charge of a multitude of HERBs as the "Grand Poobah." This is usually the person who oversees the whole organization, such as the CEO, chairman of the board, or president. (The term Grand Poobah was used on the television show *The Flintstones* as the name of a high-ranking elected official in a secret society, the Loyal Order of Water Buffaloes. The main characters, Fred Flintstone and Barney Rubble, were members of the lodge.) The Grand Poobah is who you will be looking for guidance from at a large enterprise or company. (More about the Grand Poobah in chapter 10.)

PLAYER NUMBER FOUR: SAM, HERB'S ASSISTANT.

Like HERB, Sam may or may not have a title like executive assistant, but what Sam definitely does have is practical control over HERB's calendar, itinerary, passwords, and other essentials. Sam is HERB's right-hand person, and as such they are extremely important to player number one—you. You'll be learning how to interact with Sam a little later. For now, remember that you want Sam to be your friend, you should treat Sam with respect, and you should never irritate, annoy, or anger Sam.

PLAYER NUMBER FIVE: THE DECISION INFLUENCER.

Some people make the mistake of calling this person the "Decision Maker." Wrong! All decisions about buying your stuff are technically really HERB's, and you already know why: HERB has at least 51 percent of the votes and HERB signs the contracts! Decision Influencers are important executives, with any number of titles, who are notable because a big part of their (informal) job description is to get decisions approved by HERB. They can say to HERB, "This is the person we want to work with, and here's why." They influence HERB to go your way—HERB agrees and signs the contract.

If you can't get a direct working relationship going with HERB (and very often you won't be able to), your goals for an initial call is simple: Get HERB to point you toward the Decision Influencer, and then keep HERB in the loop about everything you do with this person.

You'll be getting that advice from us in a lot of different ways, and from a lot of different angles, later in *Competitive Selling*. We repeat the point as often as we do only because we know how easy it is for salespeople to either start selling to HERB without being invited to do so (bad idea), or keep HERB out of the loop (equally bad idea).

PLAYER NUMBER SIX: THE GATEKEEPER.

This isn't Sam, unless of course you tick Sam off, in which case Sam can quickly become a Gatekeeper and a particularly impregnable barrier to HERB. The Gatekeeper isn't just the front desk person who serves as the first line of defense against unwanted calls. *Anyone* who is eager to keep you from getting through to HERB counts as a Gatekeeper.

There are likely many Gatekeepers in HERB's organization, possibly comprising a solid majority of people who work there. Your role is as an agent of change, and most of the people you run into at HERB's company fear and distrust anyone who wants to alter the status quo! This means a Gatekeeper can have a title like procurement officer, analyst, purchasing agent . . . or might even be a manager who likes things just the way they are!

This state of affairs may not be what you want to hear, may seem unfair, may make you think that the odds are stacked against you . . . but don't panic. As it turns out, once you get beyond the Gatekeeper, both HERB and Sam are *always* on the lookout for people who can help them initiate positive change in their organization. Luckily for them, you will be leapfrogging to HERB's office!

Here's a helpful hint: If what the person *does* is indicated by their title—as in purchasing agent, sales associate, travel planner, and human resources manager—and you are not calling a vice president, director, or C-level executive, you are almost certainly dealing with a Gatekeeper and are *not starting at the right person.*

There are three morals of our story (so far):

1. Don't try to sell to the Gatekeeper no matter what their title!

2. Do respectfully leapfrog over the Gatekeeper and the Decision Influencer in order to make your first sales contact with HERB's office!

3. Do get HERB to point you toward the Decision Influencer if HERB is delegating that responsibility to them. However, keep HERB in the loop about everything you do with this person.

This is the secret to competitive selling: knowing where to start and why.

ACTION STEP

Think of six to eight potentially lucrative opportunities in which you did not reach out to HERB's office first and did not win the business. It's important not to move on to the next chapter until you have thought specifically about each opportunity. Then write down the company names of the three most valuable lost opportunities.

In addition, think of your primary contact at each of those companies. You know you weren't talking to HERB first; who were you talking to first? Was it Sam, HERB's assistant? Was it the

Decision Influencer? Or were you really talking to the Gatekeeper? Remember, a manager or another employee who is resistant to change and blocking your way to HERB counts as a Gatekeeper.

CHAPTER 4

LEAPFROGGING TO HERB

At the beginning of the book we mentioned a hotel chain and an industrial supplier that became clients via calls to the VP of sales, and a multistate bank that became a client through a call to the president. These real-life success stories about great clients started when we reached out to player number two, HERB.

WHO IS HERB?

There's a HERB in every organization. As stated in the previous chapter, HERB is the decision maker we call the "51-percenter" because, in any given buying decision, we find HERB has 51 percent or more of the voting power that determines the outcome.

There are three levels of prospects you can call on in an organization. HERB is one level. The Decision Influencer who can influence HERB but doesn't sign the contract is a second level. The third level is the Gatekeeper. This person may not be who you think it is. It's not HERB's assistant or the receptionist. A true Gatekeeper in an organization is someone who is afraid of change. In many cases this person is a front-line individual or a person in a managerial role, but not an executive.

If you're a salesperson with any experience at all, we are willing to bet you already know, deep down inside, the name of the highest executive responsible for buying at your very best current account. Believe it or not, you already know who HERB is even if you did not initially call that person. You can probably picture HERB right now. HERB is the person who would have to approve, or at least accept, your chief competitor taking over that piece of business you now consider yours.

Our challenge to you is a simple one: Whenever you're calling on a brand new prospective buying organization, from this day forward, leapfrog and *start with HERB!*

We can come up with a lot of interesting reasons *not* to start with HERB, but as far as we're concerned all those reasons are excuses, and none of them really hold water. Either you want a decision or you don't. If you're a salesperson, you do. And you want to learn what that decision is sooner rather than later. That means you want the person with at least 51 percent of the voting power in the loop and, ideally, on your side.

As a general rule, those of us in sales want to spend our time, which is precious and limited, with people who can make decisions. We don't want to waste our time on those who can't. We won't repeat all the excuses we hear regarding this rule (some are pretty silly), but we will share the most popular one we hear from salespeople who don't want to start their sales process with HERB: "I tried that before and it really didn't work for [me/our

product/our service/our solution/our organization/our indus-
try/our planet]."

When we explore that response in a little more depth, what
we learn is that reaching out to HERB invariably "didn't work"
(yes, 100 percent of the time) for a very simple reason: the salesperson was trying to *sell* to HERB, typically on the first call. You'll
recall that we didn't say *sell* to HERB; we said *start* with HERB!

THE SIXTY-SECOND CHALLENGE

It's certainly true that with some accounts you can *end up*
selling to HERB. That's HERB's decision, though. And it's a decision that's not likely to come within the first sixty seconds of
the initial discussion. That's all we're challenging you about here:
your initial call, and what you do with the first sixty seconds of
that call. We're challenging you to use those sixty seconds on the
phone with HERB to make a fundamental change in your prospecting strategy. *But we are not challenging you to sell to HERB!*

Let us be absolutely clear about this. You can implement the
ideas in *Competitive Selling*; you can turn your week, your quarter, or your career around; you can make a lot more money and
have a lot more fun . . . all without ever selling to HERB. Our
challenge is simply that you *start with HERB*. That means choos-
ing to reach out to HERB's office first, identifying who you want
to call, preparing well for those critical first sixty seconds, and
then making your initial phone call to HERB's office.

Is what we're describing worth a sixty-second call? If you accept this sixty-second challenge—if you are willing to put into
practice the simple ideas you find here—we can confidently

predict that your *sales cycles will be shorter, your dead ends fewer, and your commission checks higher.*

As you will soon see for yourself, you definitely will not be asking HERB for the deal during this initial prospecting call. In fact you won't be asking HERB for any kind of commitment whatsoever. You'll be asking HERB for something very different—the one thing HERBs the world over are usually quite happy to give to total strangers: *help and guidance.*

Believe it or not, the call we are describing is not traumatic, stressful, or doomed (words salespeople typically use to describe their attempts to sell to HERB on the first call). That sixty-second call, once you get used to making it, is actually quite fun for both parties involved.

ACTION STEPS

1. Write a handwritten note to yourself that says, "Start with HERB but don't try to sell to HERB." Post it prominently.

2. Write down three advantages of starting with HERB and what they could do for your pipeline.

CHAPTER 5

BUILDING YOUR ROADMAP TO SET THE APPOINTMENT

Your first call determines whether or not you have a chance of gaining business from the person you contacted, or provides guidance to talk to someone else who is the right person. The potential value of this call should never be underestimated.

We like the observation, "Amateurs wing it—professionals plan it!" This call needs to be planned. What you want to achieve—the objective—has to be determined before you pick up the phone. And there are only two possible objectives in our prospecting system for this initial call: to set an appointment, or get guidance regarding the right person to contact. That's it. You're *not* going to get into a long conversation; you're going to respect their time and get off the phone in a very short period of time once you have accomplished one of these objectives.

There are three parts of your brain involved in this call: the survival part, the thinking part, and the emotional part. You're doing interruptive marketing. For the first seven seconds they are not listening to you. Think about answering your own phone. When it rings, what are you typically thinking? Today it's rare for people to call, so your immediate response is flight. Keep that in mind with your prospects. If you have a game plan and a roadmap, you are much less likely to end the call without accomplishing your objective! No one likes to be interrupted, so no matter what you have to offer—even if you're calling to give your prospect one million dollars—their reaction will be, "What do you want?" And they want to get you off the phone as quickly as possible.

Knowing this, you are going to honor their request and get them off the phone very quickly in order to let them get back to what they were doing. For inside sales your objective might be a bit different since you might want to do some qualifying before pursuing an appointment; but you still want to keep the conversation very short and respect the other person's time.

How do you start this call? What should you say when you get them on the phone? Most salespeople have never been taught, so they hit and miss for a while, and eventually figure out what makes the most sense. The patterns and outlines provided here reduce the frustration and help you gain more appointments in less time.

Here's what the overall process looks like for an outside sales professional on that initial phone call in order to set a first appointment:

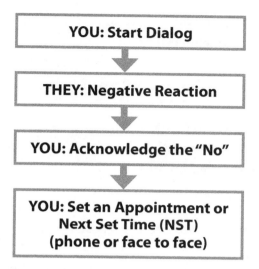

You have to say something to get a dialog started. You're actually looking for the fastest way to get the "No," because that's the first knee-jerk reaction everyone will have. So why not be prepared for it and have it rear its ugly head as soon as possible? Welcome the first no in order to get to the second. That first no is simply masking the real reason they will not meet with you or talk in greater depth. We go through the nos thoroughly in the next chapter.

As an inside sales associate, your objective might not be to set an appointment but to get a bit of information in order to start your sales process. Keep in mind that even if setting an appointment is not your objective, you are still doing interruptive marketing; so be very conscious about your prospect's time. This should not be a long conversation, but one that gives them a reason to talk with you again. Even if you're with a well-known company that your prospect is familiar with, ask yourself, "Why should they listen to what I have to say?" "What is the benefit I can provide to pique their interest?"

Let's start out with what to say to start a dialog. There is a four-part pattern to this. The pattern includes:

1. Gaining the person's attention
2. Providing a benefit
3. Stating the reason for the call
4. Closing the call

Let's break down these four parts of a call:

PART 1: When **gaining the person's attention**, the first thing to say is hello, addressing the person properly. To do this, simply mirror the way they answer the phone. If they say, "This is John," say "Good morning, John." If they say, "This is John Smith," say, "Good afternoon, John Smith." (This is the only time you will use their full name.) Should they state, "This is Mr. Smith," address them with the formal "Good morning, Mr. Smith." Should they answer the phone with "Hello" without saying their name, they are being informal with you and you can also be informal back to them:

> PROSPECT: *This is John.*
> YOU: *Good morning, John.*

PART 2: *Please do not ask, "How are you?" next!* This question indicates this is a sales call. They will put up their radar and quickly become impatient. Don't ask how they are because frankly *you don't care!* You don't care if the dog bit them, they're in a fight with their spouse, or whatever else might be happening. When you call someone you don't know, it's trite to ask "How are you?" and in many cases thwarts the conversation and blocks you from getting any further.

Instead, provide your name (always your first and last name!), your company name, and **the benefit your product or service provides**. Stating the benefit is the differentiator between you and your competition—it's what you can do to help the person you're speaking with. Can you offer something unusual or hard to find, or are you known for a specific product or locale? Are there specific insights or information you have about their industry or yours that you would like to share? It should take just one simple sentence to state the benefit and tee up the reason for the call. Try and foster some type of emotional connection between you and the person you are speaking with. Don't just concentrate on everything you can do for them.

Stacia's example: "This is Stacia Skinner from Creative Training Solutions. I don't know how familiar you are with our company—we provide customized training programs that have helped many companies improve their bottom lines."

PART 3: Next let's focus on **the reason for the call**, which is to schedule an appointment, either on the phone or face to face. It is important to know that if you are making a phone appointment with someone, be sure you say "phone appointment," not just "appointment," because the person on the other end of the line will assume you are coming in to see them.

Even if you have to qualify them, you want to get them off the phone as quickly as possible in order to respect their time.

(Inside sales professionals can refer to chapter 8, which is written with your goals in mind.)

Here's an example:

> *"The reason for my call today, John, is I'd like to set an [phone] appointment with you to discuss what you're currently doing regarding your training initiatives and share with you some observations and trends we are seeing within your industry."*

PART 4: Last, and most important, **ask for an appointment.** When you're in control of the conversation, it's not "if" you're going to get together; it's "when." Ask for a date and time to meet. Here's an example:

> *"How is Tuesday at 2:00?"*

The thought behind this concept is that people like to do business with people who are busy. Automatically you are giving the impression that you're busy.

That's it! Not overly complicated—just short, sweet, and to the point.

Keep a couple of things in mind: First, be very careful about pausing. When we say someone's name or our own name, we often pause to see if it's okay to keep going. Don't do this. You are only going to take about two minutes of their time. Your goal is to ask for an appointment and get off the phone.

Second, don't overcomplicate this process. Stick to the four-part pattern. Don't try to give the person all the information you have to offer in thirty seconds. Give them a broad-brush perspective and when you meet with them you can get into the specifics.

Third, make sure you do not say the word "needs" in your statement. Remember that the status quo is your number one competitor. If you state the word "needs" anywhere in this statement, they will latch on to that word and automatically say, "I don't need you." And frankly, they don't! Because if they did, they would be calling you. So make sure the word "needs" is nowhere to be found in your statement. You want the opportunity to show the person you are calling how you can help them with what they are currently doing.

SAY GOOD-BYE TO "OH BOTHER"

After your first call using the four-part pattern (a term we prefer to use instead of the inaccurate "script," which implies that you must recite something word for word), did you fall victim to the Winnie-the-Pooh Syndrome?

You remember Winnie-the-Pooh, of course. He's the lovable, bumbling bear who always seems to be wandering aimlessly through the Hundred Acre Wood. Whenever Pooh runs into any kind of obstacle he doesn't quite understand (which is pretty regularly), he says one phrase almost automatically: "Oh bother."

Eliminating the Winnie-the-Pooh Syndrome is the most common challenge salespeople face when they first use the four-part pattern. They apologize way too much and seem to wander aimlessly through their own "Hundred Acre Wood." You don't want to sound like Winnie-the-Pooh. Any phrase that remotely resembles any of the following must be edited out of your pattern:

- ▪ "I'm so sorry to bother you."
- ▪ "I don't mean to be a bother, but . . . "
- ▪ "If it isn't too much of a bother, could I ask you to . . . ?"

You don't have to actually use the word *bother* to come across with the same basic Pooh attitude of tentativeness and perpetual apology. The person you are calling already has enough encounters with people like this during the day, so you should also edit out wording like:

- ▪ "I'm sorry to [bug/disturb/interrupt] you."
- ▪ "I shouldn't have to ask you this, but . . . "
- ▪ "I hope I'm not calling you at a bad time."
- ▪ "Is this a bad time to talk?"
- ▪ "Is this a good time to talk?"

Be aware of words such as *perhaps, hope,* and *maybe* as well, and of offering alternative meeting times. Your approach should be confident, but not pushy; focused, but not arrogant; direct, but not rude. This leaves no room for Winnie-the-Pooh. Make sure your tone projects that you are not afraid and that you have a purpose and a right to call.

Keep polishing what you will say until all evidence of the silly old bear has been completely erased. Practice makes perfect, so do it now!

ACTION STEPS

1. Write your roadmap for the initial call. Make sure you include a benefit statement to show the person you're speaking to why they should listen to you. Then practice. Practice with others. Call your own voicemail and record yourself to see if you would make an appointment with yourself.

2. Take time to write down any "Oh bother" statements you use and commit to removing them from your calling pattern.

3. When looking at your roadmap for the initial call, make sure you do not have the word "needs" in any part of the statement.

CHAPTER 6

HOLY CRAP! HERE COME THE "NO"S!

Marisa's story: "I remember making a call early in my business to a VP of sales. I opened confidently with the reason for my call and his first response was, 'I have thirty sales books on my desk, Marisa. I read a new sales book every month and teach it back to my sales team. In addition, I was the first of forty salespeople in this company and no one is in a better position to train my sales team than me.' I attempted, unsuccessfully at first, to acknowledge the no, sharing with him how it is nice to have an outside voice like mine reinforce what he's teaching.

"That reasoning actually did not work and he asked me to call back in the future; there was no interest right now. I did, and continued to make purposeful calls to him over the next six months. One day, out of the blue, I got an email asking me what I would charge to work with his new hires. That gave me a foot in the door to an account that eventually became my top customer and was for seven years in a row."

The morals of the story are: First, just because you get a no on the first call does not mean it will be a no forever. Don't stop too soon! Timing is part of the sales process. If you feel what you have to offer can help your prospect, don't be a pest but be persistent. Competitive sellers don't give up quickly. And second, you should always be ready for knee-jerk objections to come flying at you by knowing what the top objections will be. They shouldn't come as a surprise. Anticipate and prepare answers for them.

There's a difference between impulsive responses and real objections in the sales process. The approach for addressing prospecting objections is different from that of addressing objections you hear when you're deeper in the sale. In this chapter we are focused on arming you specifically for prospecting objections.

It would be great if every time you used the four-part dialog pattern you always got a yes. But you're still going to get the no (and holy crap we hear that a lot!). Negative impulsive responses are always to be anticipated. Each time you get on the phone, anticipate that you will receive a no coming at you at ninety miles an hour. All no responses fall into four categories:

1. I'm okay
2. Not interested
3. Too busy
4. Redirecting questions or statements

Here's another pattern to help you to handle these objections:

1. Take down their guard.
2. Repeat their concern.
3. Reassure.
4. Resume.

This pattern keeps you in control of the call and at the same time shows your prospect you are listening. You never want to put your prospect on the defensive or give them the impression you think they have made a stupid decision.

Now we'll discuss how to acknowledge the no and find out the reason behind it. Just like your prospect, we all react impulsively when someone objects. Your natural impulse is to ask a question, which immediately puts your prospect on the defensive. Think of their "guard" as being at level ten out of ten and their interest being at level zero. Your goal is to take down that guard and immediately disarm them. The taking-down-the-guard statement can be anything from "I completely understand" or "I appreciate that" or "That's okay" to "That's perfectly fine." Your disarming tone and timing (not freezing in flight mode!) make a huge difference, even more so than getting every word right.

Think about going into a retail store. You walk in and the sales clerk asks, "May I help you?" Your first reaction, whether you need the clerk or not, is to put up your guard and say "No, just looking." Seven seconds later your guard goes down and you realize you need them, but now they're nowhere to be found. The same goes for your prospect. Their phone rings unexpectedly, they answer, and their impulse is to go into defensive mode and just say no.

Let's look at some examples:

1. I'm okay: *"We are happy with XYZ Company."*

> You say, *"I can appreciate that. [Take down their guard.] Other companies I work with also use XYZ Company [Repeat their concern] and we find that we can enhance what they provide. [Reassure.] That's why I would like to*

get together with you. [Resume.] How about we get together and talk further. How does your schedule look for Tuesday at 2:00?"

Enhance is a wonderful word because it's nonthreatening. You never want to get into a position in which the person you are calling feels like they have to put up their dukes! During this call, you are not trying to take anything away from what they are currently doing. Other words that work nicely are *supplement, enrich, complement,* and *an addition to.* If you cannot "enhance" due to the nature of the product or service you provide, can you be a secondary resource? Most companies deal with more than one vendor so they have a backup in case something happens, and wouldn't you rather get a little bit of something than a little bit of nothing? Sometimes getting a foot in the door is all you need.

2. Not interested: *"Thank you for the call but I am really not interested."*

> You say, *"That's okay. Some of my best customers stated they weren't interested at first until they really saw the **benefits** of what we have to offer. That's why I would like to get together with you. How does your schedule look on Tuesday at 2:00?"*

Or your prospect might say, "You are too expensive for our company." Anything dealing with price is an impulsive response. It really falls into the "not interested" category.

> You say, *"I appreciate your sharing that with me. As a matter of fact, some of my current customers thought the same*

thing initially, until they saw how we could work within their budgets and provide a benefit to their companies. How about we get together and have a conversation? How does your schedule look for Tuesday at 2:00?"

Don't get into a discussion about why they think you are expensive. Disarm their knee-jerk response by showing them you were listening. Other words you can use instead of *benefits* are *advantages, asset, additional resource,* and *additional perk.*

3. Too busy: *"I'm busy right now; I'm running out the door."*

When your prospect says they're too busy, they're assuming you want to have a long conversation. Unless you are in inside sales, you only want to set the appointment and get off the phone. That's why you're avoiding "Is this a good time?" It sends the message that you need a lot of time. But you don't.

Your impulse is to ask what's a good time to call back, but that doesn't result in their revealing the real reason for putting you off. Here's what works:

"I understand you're busy. The only reason I'm contacting you is to set an appointment for a future date. How does your schedule look for Tuesday at 2:00?"

As a result, you will get the real reason they said they were busy, and you are armed to address that when you hear it. Or, since you did not do what most salespeople do and try to product-dump all over them in thirty seconds, they recognize that you showed them respect by listening to their response, and set an appointment with you!

4. Redirecting questions or statements: *"Can you give me an idea of your pricing?" "Can you send me something?" "Can you call me at the end of the quarter?"*

All of these questions are attempts to redirect the call in order to find a reason to hang up. Remember, even these questions are impulsive reactions. The difference here is you are going to redirect or position their question or statement in order to gain control of the conversation and get back to the original purpose of your call, which is to set an appointment.

At this point you ask a question to gain back control. The first part is "I'm just curious . . . " or "Before I get you off the phone, I'm just curious . . . "; and the second part starts with "How . . . " or "What . . . " This is your autopilot for steering the conversation in the right direction. Fall back on these questions if you get stuck on how to address an impulsive response, because they can be used for any type of response you get.

The key here is that the one who asks the question is the one who's in control. When your prospect asks a question, they want control of the conversation or to end it by hanging up. The questions you ask are really saying, "Hold on a minute—let me tell you why we should continue."

Here's an example of how this works:

YOUR PROSPECT: *So give me an idea of how much this would cost.*

YOU: *I can appreciate that cost is a concern. I can assure you we are cost competitive, and depending on your circumstances I'm sure we can accommodate you. However, **before***

I get you off the phone, I'm just curious . . . what types of widgets are you currently using?

YOUR PROSPECT: *We use ABC Company for this.*

YOU: *That's exactly why we should meet, since we can enhance what ABC Company provides. I would really like to show you how. How does your schedule look on Tuesday at 2:00?*

Your question steers the conversation back to your original purpose and gives you control of the conversation. Your prospect will demonstrate what's called *answer reflex*: you ask a question and they automatically answer you because you're in control of the conversation.

Let's look at another example:

YOUR PROSPECT: *Can you email or send me information? or Can you give me your website address?*

(Again, this is a perfect opportunity to redirect the conversation.)

YOU: *I can appreciate your wanting me to [email or send information/give you our website address] and I can definitely do that for you. However, before I do, and to get a better understanding of what to send, I'm just curious . . . what are you currently doing regarding your XYZ process?*

YOUR PROSPECT: *We use ABC Company for that.*

YOU: *That's exactly why we should get together so I can show you how we can [enhance what you're doing now/be a secondary resource for you]. How does your schedule look for Tuesday at 2:00?*

If your prospect gives you the exact same negative response twice . . . *stop!* They are indicating that no matter what you say, this is not a time for them to think about what you have to offer. You then steer the conversation to a later date when you will call at their convenience.

It sounds like this:

YOUR PROSPECT: *Can you call me at the end of the quarter?*

YOU: *I'm happy to do so, but **before we get off the phone, I'm just curious . . . what's** happening between now and the end of the quarter?* (Tone is critical here! Be sincere.)

YOUR PROSPECT: *I'm actually doing budgets and have no time to talk right now.*

YOU: *I appreciate that, and actually many of our customers have seen the benefits we can provide during the budgeting process. Let's get together so I can show you how we can help. How does your schedule look Tuesday at 2:00?*

YOUR PROSPECT: *I really cannot commit at this time. These budgets are consuming all of my time.*

YOU: *I respect your time. Why don't I contact you on [a date in the future] and we can set an appointment at that time?*

YOUR PROSPECT: *Sure that will be fine.*

Most people think you won't contact them on that future date because the number-one failure of salespeople is lack of follow-through. Later in *Competitive Selling* we'll discuss what to say when you contact your prospect on the future date, and you will get the appointment more times than not!

The initial phone conversation is that easy! Does it take practice? Yes! Does it work every time you get a prospect on the phone? No! Nothing works 100 percent of the time. But what if you could increase your appointments by just 5 to 10 percent? What would that do for your bottom line? It's the small changes that can make the biggest difference. Try it. You might be surprised by the end result.

ACTION STEP

Make a list of the top five negative responses you hear on a consistent basis and write your responses in your own words. Make sure you write them in your speaking voice, not your writing voice.

Practice, Practice, Practice. This is the most critical part of the call. If you cannot get past the first "no", you will not set the appointment.

CHAPTER 7

GAINING AN APPOINTMENT WHEN CANVASSING

To this point we've focused exclusively on phone strategies that can earn you an initial contact with HERB, Sam, or the Decision Influencer. Here is another tactic that is potentially just as powerful as that telephone discussion: *canvassing*. This is a strategy exclusively designed to lay the groundwork for future discussions. It can deliver astonishing results if you are willing to follow some simple guidelines.

We've trained field salespeople from just about every industry you can think of to do this kind of canvassing. Many of them approached it deeply skeptical that it had anything to do with their sales process, but they became true believers when they found out for themselves how easily they can use these ideas to engage the right person.

Everything to do with canvassing happens face to face, and the initial conversation unfolds not with HERB, Sam, or the Decision Influencer, but with the receptionist of the building, the front desk person, or player number five, the Gatekeeper. For simplicity we'll call this the receptionist in this chapter.

In case you're not familiar with the term *canvass* as it's used here, it means "to seek or solicit support by means of a personal visit." For our purposes, the "support" during this visit comes, in virtually all cases, from the receptionist, and not from anyone else.

You read that correctly: Your job is to win over the receptionist you meet for the very first time when you walk into the lobby. The success of your canvassing efforts will not, however, depend on your ability to *sell* to this person, or to anyone else.

This bears repeating: ***You are not trying to sell anything during this visit!*** Rather, your success depends on your ability to establish rapport with the receptionist and get a clear commitment from them that the right person will in fact receive your carefully assembled package of information. This package, which is designed to pique HERB or the Decision Influencer's curiosity, is what motivates them to take your call a few days later. It's cold calling in person.

We're not talking about investing an entire day going from one building to the next searching for receptionists you can talk to. Managing your precious time is extremely important. The kind of canvassing we're talking about is an easy, low-risk, high-return way to maximize your time in the field *when you are already out on an appointment*. Be sure to execute what follows with that in mind. Here's the process:

1. Use the tactics you've learned so far to set one or two appointments in a given area.

2. While you're in the neighborhood make use of your downtime before, between, or after appointments to canvass new companies by dropping off curiosity-piquing information destined for new HERBs.

3. Follow up by telephone with those new connections one to three days later (max) to get your all-important referral names.

Here's the good news: You *do not* need to know the identity of the HERB in question in order to pass your information along and get great results from the tactics detailed here.

Curious about how it works? Sure you are. Read on!

CANVASSING CRITERIA

Just so you are completely clear about this process, the kind of canvassing suggested here definitely *does not* involve trying to get on-the-spot face time with HERB or Sam or anyone except the receptionist. If you pressure them to meet with HERB, Sam, or anyone else right then, you're missing the point; and if you attempt to close a deal on the spot, you're missing the point!

You should show up unannounced at a company that meets these criteria:

▪ The company is located within easy walking or driving distance of a scheduled appointment. This is so you won't stand someone up if you get distracted by your canvassing conversation. Leave yourself enough time to disengage and make your scheduled commitment with plenty of time to spare.

▪ The facility is open to the public. No stalking. No creative tricks for getting in the door. There should be easy public access to the front desk.

Stacia's story: "A word to the wise—don't stay away from a business that looks too small. The size of a building can sometimes be deceiving. I once walked into a building that looked tiny from the outside, but when I followed up with HERB, they had more than twenty salespeople working remotely. Don't judge a book by its cover!"

WHAT TO DO AHEAD OF TIME

At least *one day before* your scheduled canvassing slots, complete a few essential preliminary steps as follows:

1. Confirm the general area where you will be canvassing.

2. Spend ten or fifteen minutes using online resources to locate the best virtual tour of the area you'll be visiting. You can download the free Google Earth software and, in many cities, use the "Street View" function to get an astonishingly clear look at the area. Identify any promising locations and record the addresses.

3. Determine the likely title or titles of the HERBs at the target organizations you'll be canvassing. (As someone

who sells sales training, Stacia almost always asks for the VP of sales.) Do *not* spend a lot of time trying to research who HERB is online. It's too easy to waste time this way, and you will find that the people you talk to in person tend to be quite helpful when it comes to pointing you toward HERB. Of course, if you happen to come across a likely name or title, go ahead and jot it down.

4. Pull together a *minimal* amount of printed information to leave at each company. It should be just enough to whet HERB's appetite, yet not so much that HERB concludes that no further discussion is necessary. *Do not* include any pricing information in any of the materials you distribute.

5. Everything you prepare should be placed inside a sealed envelope. You don't want the receptionist reviewing your materials and deciding whether or not they will pass your information along. Without a sealed envelope you're taking a chance that your materials will never make it past the front desk! Put the company's name and HERB's name (if you have it) on the front of the envelope. If you don't know HERB's name, write the title of the HERB you want the envelope to go to.

6. Have your business card ready. It can either be attached to your envelope or separate from it, but it must be readily available when you walk in the door.

YOUR PURPOSE

You're not yet ready to walk in the door and start canvassing because you don't yet know the exact purpose of your visit. It's just as important to understand why you are canvassing as it is to understand why you are picking up the telephone to call HERB's office! You're canvassing to confirm HERB's name, title, and direct phone number . . . and drop off some information.

And that's all you are doing! You are not trying to speak directly with HERB, Sam, or anyone else other than the receptionist. You are not trying to qualify the opportunity, and of course you are not trying to sell. Let us repeat that: *You are not trying to sell.* The single most common way salespeople self-destruct when canvassing is that they forget the purpose of their visit and start trying to push for a meeting or a decision. If you do this, you will have wasted all your preparation time, all your time on the visit, and a big investment of your energy!

Again, your goals are to confirm HERB's name, title, and phone number, and drop off your envelope.

As you might expect, the receptionist is the person you need to help you reach HERB.

YOUR PLAN FOR INTERACTING WITH THE RECEPTIONIST

The elements for dealing effectively with the receptionist when you show up in person parallel the ones you use when you encounter Gatekeepers on the phone. They are:

- Be polite.
- Ask for help.
- Be specific about the purpose of your visit.

▪ Maintain control of the conversation.

▪ Once you have obtained the desired information and dropped off your envelope, simply leave the building.

Beyond these five directives (which align with everything you've learned so far), use common sense in all your interactions with the receptionist. This means not pretending you know HERB when you don't, not copping an attitude, not using an aggressive or otherwise inappropriate tone or body language, and not saying anything you're likely to regret later.

With these essential points addressed, you are ready to tackle what to say to the receptionist.

WHAT TO SAY TO THE RECEPTIONIST

What follows is the basic pattern for your discussion with the receptionist during a canvassing visit. You don't have to recite it verbatim, and you shouldn't. This should be something you internalize and use in a flexible, spontaneous way to project authenticity and establish rapport with this person.

Having said that, we want to caution you *not* to make radical changes to the pattern outlined below. Covering the points, in the order provided, using the tone suggested, *works*, and you shouldn't stray too far from the pattern:

▪ Gaining their Attention
▪ Reason for the visit
▪ Closing statement

Begin by glancing at the receptionist's nameplate or nametag, if you can see it. Use their actual name when you introduce yourself, because that makes the exchange more personal. Be careful, though, to phrase their name as a question. That way, if for some reason you've gotten the name wrong, or you're pronouncing it wrong, or the person is not the one whose nameplate is on the desk, they'll be more likely to volunteer their correct name and you can maintain rapport:

1. Gaining Their Attention:

> *"Good morning—Riley? [Riley nods or responds with a correction.] My name is Stacia Skinner from Creative Training Solutions. I'm hoping you can help me."*

People love to help, and with this simple, powerful request you've immediately lowered their guard!

2. Reason for the visit:

> *"I need to get this information to your vice president of sales [or whatever title you are targeting]. Would you be so kind as to make sure they receive it?"*

Or:

> *"It's important that I get this information in front of your vice president of sales [or whatever title you are targeting]. Can you make sure this gets into their hands?"*

Almost every single time, Riley will give you an immediate positive response to this request.

3. Closing statement:

> *"Thank you so much. Can you provide me with the name of the person you will be forwarding this to so I can follow up with them?"*

Usually you'll get a quick, positive response to this request as well. Assuming the conversation is going well, you should continue with:

> *"I really appreciate your help. You wouldn't happen to have [his/her] phone number or extension, would you?"*

If the exchange is going well, get the full name of the receptionist as well as that of HERB. You can write it down as soon as you get out the door. (It's nice to have, but not essential.)

That's it! The whole exchange should take you less than two minutes. Pass along your envelope, confirm HERB's name and title, get the direct phone number if possible, and *move on*. You have just leapfrogged to HERB!

THE FOLLOW-UP CALL

The timing part of your follow-up call is important. Call HERB one to three days after the canvassing visit—the sooner the better. Your objective during the call is to get help and guidance from HERB and nothing else. This might be very different from what you're doing now. When you make that call, remember to mention the name of the person you gave your envelope to and the date you did so. *Do not, under any circumstance, ask,* "Did you receive the information I dropped off?" This makes you sound like an interrogator and gets your conversation off on the wrong foot.

Below is an outline of what you should say during that call, using Marisa as an example. Again, feel free to personalize it so that it feels natural to you, but don't change the essence of what this pattern covers. Stick to the same points.

> *Good morning, John. This is Marisa Pensa from Methods in Motion.*
>
> *I don't know if you're familiar with our company, but we provide customized sales training for a wide range of industries. I stopped by your office on [date] and left some information with [name] in your reception area.*
>
> *I am hoping you can help me. I'm looking for the person who is in charge of your sales training for your company, and I'm hoping you can give me some guidance as to who that would be.*

You are wondering why I am not asking for an appointment with HERB. The reason is simple. I don't want to assume the person I am speaking with is the right person. My first encounter was with the receptionist. I cannot assume she gave me HERB. In some companies, the receptionist is told that if anyone walks in asking for a particular person, they are to direct them to someone who has nothing to do with what the person asking for them does. However, should this be the HERB you want, steer the conversation to gain the appointment.

KEEPING HERB IN YOUR NETWORK

Once you have found the true HERB (perhaps you are referred to a better HERB), and have locked in HERB as an ally,
how can you make sure you keep HERB in your network? There
are three ideas we would like to share with you on this point—
each simple, direct, and virtually free. If you follow all three, you
will stand a very good chance of turning a short-term, transac-
tional business relationship with HERB into a long-term alliance
that benefits both parties. Here they are:

1. **Don't bother HERB with the small stuff, but do keep
    HERB in the loop on the big stuff.** Some salespeople
    have complicated this simple idea by sending HERB
    micro-updates on virtually every single event that
    happens in the selling cycle! Don't do this. HERB
    already has too many people competing for their
    attention. Wait for the big events like the launch of your
    program or the first truly big win you post on behalf
    of HERB's organization. Be sure to keep your updates
    brief!

2. **Send HERB a handwritten note or an email monthly,
    quarterly, or somewhere in between as appropriate.**
    This is particularly important if HERB's organization
    decides, for whatever reason, that the time is not yet
    right to buy from you. You have worked hard to find
    this opening; don't abandon it just because you didn't
    immediately get the short-term decision you were
    after. Keep your notes brief, friendly, and focused on
    the future. If you had a good series of discussions with

Sam, HERB's assistant, you might want to send them a note from time to time as well. A perfect reason to write a note or email is if you see something new is happening in their company or industry. Just saying congratulations or "I was thinking of you" keeps you top of mind.

3. **Ask to connect online.** There are lots of people who use LinkedIn and other social networks for sales and business-related networking purposes. We recommend you ask for HERB's LinkedIn contact, as it's the most comfortable online connection for sales business. It's a truly amazing resource, and if you haven't taken advantage of it yet, you really should. After your first or second good conversation with HERB, suggest the two of you join each other's LinkedIn networks. You just never know who will benefit, or how, from that connection!

ACTION STEPS

1. Look at your calendar and map out where you will be in the next few days. Check out the area on Google Earth with Street View. See what companies are nearby and pick three to canvass.

2. In anticipation of your next canvassing opportunity in the field, complete the preliminary tasks discussed in this chapter.

3. Practice the canvassing pattern you learned in this chapter. Say it out loud until it comes naturally to you and you can say it so it sounds like *your own words.*

CHAPTER 8

ENGAGING OVER THE PHONE FOR INSIDE SALES

THE PROCESS AND ART OF SELLING OVER THE PHONE

When you engage in an inside sales world, there are a lot of similarities to outside sales but also some distinct differences. In outside sales you have a lot of props to help you. You see photos in peoples' offices and have easier access to creating icebreakers. There is a certain established trust that happens simply by being face to face. To be effective over the phone, you have to have a very tight process that holds someone's attention. You are vying for thirty more seconds of their time and need enough enthusiasm, personality, and chameleon-like adaptability to keep the person tuned in.

Marisa's story: "A company in the business products industry was struggling to grow sales. They had fifteen outside salespeople with heavy books of business, and prospecting was just not happening often enough.

"Sarah, a customer service representative, knew she had the capacity (and desire) to help drive sales, but she only had a couple of spare hours a day. She was unique compared to the rest of her team, as she was eager to try something brand new. Sarah spent about a month working with our Methods in Motion trainers on her prospecting and follow-up calls. Even though she had no previous sales experience, she secured twelve new accounts in just forty-five days.

"This really excited her colleagues. If Sarah could make this impact in forty-five days, using only two hours a day, what could they do with a full-time commitment? As a result, the company hired three full-time inside salespeople to really capitalize on their inside sales. They used the inside sales prospecting approach laid out in this chapter to grow accounts and steadily gain new accounts for their organization."

Stacia's Story: "A large hospitality company needed the ability to capture smaller accounts. They had an outside team but there were select accounts that did not justify the time commitment needed for outside sales calls. So they decided to create an inside sales team. They hired eight people to handle inside sales. Creative Training Solutions trained them on how to handle both inbound and outbound calls. In a matter of just a few months their sales were 75 percent higher than what had been projected for this new department."

There are many other examples that reinforce the simple fact that *inside sales work*. But we would be remiss if we did not address the growing need for inside sales professionals to be well skilled and to have the resources needed to win. Inside sales can be a tremendous way to grow a business.

Sure, there are challenges to inside sales. We can't see the prospect or customer. We can look them up on a social network but we lose valuable body language. In fact, 55 percent of communication is body language, so that leaves 38 percent for how we say it—our tone, cadence, and enthusiasm—and 7 percent for the words we use. But the benefits far outweigh the challenges.

GAINING A COMPETITIVE ADVANTAGE OVER THE PHONE

To counteract some of the challenges, position yourself to gain a competitive advantage and be better at it than your competition. And not just a little better; you need to be someone your prospect or client wants to talk to again. You must be memorable.

To be memorable, call your prospect back on time so time doesn't kill the deal. Breathe life back into the opportunity and bring the prospect right back to your last conversation quickly. We want you to follow a documented sales process, but you're not a robot . . . far from it. You make it *you* and it feels completely natural.

In an inside world, "phone sales warriors" need to deliberately work harder to build trust and relationships. Even mastering your customer relations management software and the multiple applications you have minimized and need to address throughout the day can drive up your ability to pound the phones. And "pound the phones" can look totally different for each person reading this chapter.

Marisa's story: "I pound the phones in my own business one to two hours at a time. I turn off email, silence my phone, and focus on nothing but dialing and new business development. Others might need to do that several times throughout the day in set increments. Nothing increases our paychecks faster than prospecting for new business, either with brand new clients or existing customers."

Getting back to the A x E = R concept from chapter 2, since the A, or activity part of the equation, is a decision, we'll concentrate on improving the E part of the equation, your efficiency over the phone, by addressing what works and what doesn't work in phone sales.

THE GOAL OF ENGAGING IN PHONE SALES

The goal of outside sales is to set a face-to-face appointment, which is your NST (next set time). You also want an appointment in inside sales, but that requires that you extend the conversation, pique your prospect's interest, qualify them, and learn a little about them on the phone *before* setting that appointment. There are exceptions to this in some industries in which going for the appointment immediately is the right approach, so discuss this with your team to determine which approach is better for your business.

But for most inside sales, you need "meat" on that first call or future calls. If not, you will be screened and forwarded to voicemail land, and you'll never be connected with the prospect again. Unlike outside sales where you can simply show up in the prospect's office for your follow-up meeting, relationships that are 100-percent over the phone require more engagement on the first call. Establishing a strong level of interest will reduce the chances of being forwarded into voicemail. Let's look at how this works, starting with a receptionist.

TIPS FOR ENGAGING WITH A RECEPTIONIST

Another distinction between outside and inside sales is how to connect with the receptionist. In inside sales you often find yourself talking to the receptionist far more than HERB, Sam, or the Decision Influencer. They can quickly become your friend or your foe.

Make it a rule of thumb to interview the receptionist, but don't ask more than two questions per call. The delivery of your questions matters. Phrases like those below will take down their guard by not sounding too abrasive. (These phrases are not needed as much in person but are essential for disarming a receptionist.)

"Jane, just so I'm better prepared when I speak with John, do you happen to know . . . "

"Just out of curiosity . . . "

"By the way . . . "

"You wouldn't happen to know . . . "

Here is an example:

"Good morning, Jane. This is Marisa Pensa from Methods in Motion. I am hoping you can help me. I am looking for your vice president of sales. Could you help me understand who this would be?"

Jane says: "Sure, that's John."

"Thank you so much, Jane. Just so I'm better prepared when I do speak with John, I noticed you have one location on your website. Is this the only location you currently have?"

When you gain information, be gracious and show your appreciation! So many salespeople don't do this simple thing. Let the person know you truly appreciate their help!

YOUR ROADMAP FOR ENGAGING HERB, SAM, OR THE DECISION INFLUENCER

When you get connected with HERB, Sam, or the Decision Influencer, these are your goals for the initial discussion:

- ▪ Communicate clearly the reason for your call and what's in it for them.
- ▪ Acknowledge the impulsive negative response.
- ▪ Confirm their function in the company to be sure you're speaking to the right person.
- ▪ Find out something of value to this person's role that differentiates you from the competition.
- ▪ Verify the decision-making process.

■ Build rapport. (Remember, inside sales requires you to be memorable!) Can you learn something about their family, occupation, or recreation?

■ Summarize the call, stating back to them what you heard and exactly where your company can provide value.

■ Set an appointment—or as we refer to it, a *next set time.*

Here's a call in action:

[Open with credibility and what's in it for them.]

"Hi John. This is Marisa Pensa with Methods in Motion. I was pointed specifically in your direction and I'm not sure how familiar you are with us. We are an industry leader in hands-on inside sales training. You might be familiar with us from attending an event or one of our webinars. Just curious . . . does our name ring a bell?"

[Ask a very brief question (Just curious . . . does our name ring a bell?) to engage the prospect, and so they can answer it as briefly as possible, then quickly move to the reason for the call.]

"The reason for my call is that we've been working with a lot of businesses that are very similar to yours, really helping them reduce the frustrations of _____ and _____."

[Now transition to questioning]

> *"Today I would like to get a better feel for how your com-*
> *pany handles those things and share some ideas about how*
> *we may be able to help. By the way . . . "*

We can't completely script this conversation because it's a *conversation*. But you can be well prepared for where the questions will go and know your first three questions cold. The key is to **earn the right to ask questions.**

Opening the call with value and a clear statement of what's in it for them, what type of problems you solve, and/or why they should take the time to talk to you creates an environment for your prospect to be more open to your questions.

By the end of the first call you will likely know if you can get that person to take your call again.

THE FOLLOW-UP PROCESS

For phone sales warriors out there, the sales process is rarely a one-call close. You don't have the luxury of sitting across the table from someone over coffee with a notepad and their full attention. You *earn* every single minute—even every single second—especially during the first call. If they don't find the first call valuable, they can easily screen your next one.

Your company's story should be deliberately told in pieces over a series of calls, adding something new and valuable each time you speak with your prospect. You can actually build relationships faster through a series of five-minute phone calls than you can by trying to have one awesome thirty-minute phone call. The thirty-minute call can feel like a huge win, and maybe it is. But be careful. The long call might be memorable for you, but it might set you up to get screened the next time. How much of your thirty-minute call do you think your prospect is going to remember, especially if most of it was you talking?

There are certainly exceptions to every rule, but don't force-feed your company's entire story to your prospect in one phone call. Aim for your first call to be brief, and cover the key points that are important to your industry. Think of the rest of the sales process as a series of "touches" made over a set period of time after the first call (with some exceptions particular to certain industries), to go from "Hello" through a natural progression in which they start doing business with you and keep doing so. Here is an analogy of this process:

Marisa's story: "As I write today, my family is making chili on a nice fall day. The house smells wonderful. We love fall where we live in the South. Troy, who is in charge of the cooking, is meticulous about his chili—the ingredients, the timing, and the phases of its development. He explains there are three sets of seasonings that give the chili a complex flavor. In my simple mind, we should just be able to dump it all in at the same time. It would be done much faster, you know . . . but that's not how he makes chili. There is group one of key ingredients, then an hour later group two, and then two hours later group three. Each ingredient matters, and so does the timing of when he adds them to develop the masterpiece of great chili."

So it is with phone sales. You shouldn't dump it all in by telling them everything on the first call. You also shouldn't short-cut or fast-track results, skipping the timing required to let the recipe properly develop. It just won't work and it's too much to absorb at once.

Layer your conversations. Leave your prospect with two points of value and new flavoring in each call to whet their appetite for more. Don't call again the next day, but don't wait three weeks either. Timing is everything.

It's a proven fact that whether it's outside or inside sales, you need to "touch" your prospect a number of times. This is true in a cold-call world and applies even to winning back old customers. The touches are not just via phone, not just via email, and not just via social media. You really want to marry a variety of communication techniques to gain a competitive edge.

Does it take practice? Yes! Does it work every time you get someone on the phone? No! Nothing works 100 percent of the time, just as in outside sales. But here again, what if you could increase your qualified and interested prospects by 5 to 10 percent? What would that do for your bottom line? Again, it's the small changes you make that can make the biggest difference. Try the patient approach and reap the rewards!

ACTION STEPS

1. Write out your starting dialog along with the first question you will ask your prospect. Be sure to practice this so you can always re-create a natural flow of dialog.

2. Once you have mastered the dialog and first question, write down the first three questions you will ask when you have earned the right to ask more questions. Again, create the flow and make it natural.

CHAPTER 9

WARM AND FUZZY CALLS

Marisa's story: "Suzy is talking to Matt, a long-time customer. They have excellent rapport. She knows his kids' names, where they went on their last vacation, their dog's name, and even that they have a fish tank. Matt purchases only a small portion of what Suzy has to offer. They have a great conversation; it lasts thirty minutes. After the call she realizes that oops—there is a huge push this month to grow product ABC, and Matt doesn't buy that product from her. There is even a bonus tied to it!"

How often do you get off a "warm call" having forgotten the objective? It takes just as much preparation to make a warm call effective as it does those not-so-warm calls that we discussed earlier.

We cover three types of warm calls in this chapter:

1. Calling existing, regularly buying accounts to upsell and cross-sell

2. Reactivating dormant accounts
3. Following up on prospecting calls when you were asked to call at a later date

Picture yourself dining with your family at your favorite restaurant. You have finished your meal and the server approaches to offer dessert and asks, "Did you guys save room for dessert?" Everyone around the table collectively moans about being too full and no one orders dessert.

Now let's picture a different scenario: The server approaches and says enthusiastically, "We have a brand new locally made dessert selection. Our most popular item right now is the summer bourbon apple pound cake with caramel topping. It's great for sharing and I could bring one for the table. We have three other amazing options if you'd like to take a look. I'm assuming you saved just enough room for a little treat, right?"

There's a good chance someone at the table will be enticed to order a dessert when it's offered that way—and they might not even want to share!

The same concept applies to opening a call with an existing customer and following up on an initial meeting or conversation. There is no disputing that dead-end openings produce dead-end (and revenue killing) responses.

Before we get into the right way to phrase the opening of these warm calls, let's talk about the wrong way. There are three dead-end openings that are persistently used by sales professionals, whether the call is to a current customer or a potential customer. We hear them and we know you hear them, too. They are:

1. "Just checking in"
2. "Just following up"
3. "Just touching base"

To be clear, we are not asking you to remove these words from your sales vocabulary completely, but when you follow such phrases with " . . . to see if you need anything" or " . . . to see what you decided," you are absolutely talking your way into a dead end. It will most likely be followed by, "Nah, we're good right now." (Just like "No thanks. We are too full for dessert.")

Now let's look at openings to use instead. The process is similar to what we covered earlier; we're simply tweaking the wording to adjust to the nature of the warm call. First make sure you clearly identify who you are and the purpose of your call. This is still interruptive marketing, even to an existing customer, so don't assume they know who you are or what company you're with.

When speaking with an existing customer you have personally spoken to before, it's okay (and encouraged) to ask them how they are doing next. Because you care! This is not a cold call. If you're calling an existing account and you are the new contact who has never spoken with them before, your roadmap is more closely tied to the four-part pattern for starting dialog discussed earlier. You don't know them and you don't have a relationship with them even though they are a customer of your company.

Here is Marisa's pattern for upselling and cross-selling an active client:

"Good morning, John. This is Marisa Pensa with Methods in Motion. How is your Friday going so far? By the way,

thank you again for your trust in us and for giving us your business. We really do appreciate it!

"The reason for my call today is I was looking at your account and realized there are some opportunities you're not taking advantage of that I think would really make sense for your business. I'd like to set an appointment with you to discuss this in further detail. How does your schedule look for Tuesday at 2:00?"

The reason to ask for an appointment is to distinguish a "Howdy" call from a sales call. It's okay to call to thoughtfully inquire about a customer's vacation or surgical procedure—that's good for the relationship! But this is a sales call, so you want to ask for an appointment to get additional business.

Here is Stacia's story about reactivating a dormant account:

"Way back in my early days of training, I called on a client who had done quite a bit of business with the company I was selling for, in the past but had just stopped. I decided to ask if we had done something wrong. When he answered, 'Yes, your company did do something wrong,' I apologized and told him I wanted to discuss this further and show him that we had changed. He cut me off and said, 'I really think this would be a waste of time.'

"I confidently stated that I felt it wouldn't be. I asked him to give me the opportunity to meet with him and his colleagues to hear their story and tell mine. After a brief pause he agreed. After meeting with them and showing them how we would be different, they became a repeat client for many

years after. Just because something went wrong in the past doesn't mean you cannot win them back!"

Every company has a different definition of a dormant account. For our purposes, it is a client whose normal buying process has become stagnant. They might be your account or you might be their new sales representative.

Here is Stacia's pattern for calling about a dormant account:

> *"Hi John. This is Stacia Skinner with Creative Training Solutions. [If you are new, state that you are new to the account.] The reason for my call is I was looking at your account and realized we haven't heard from you in some time. I'm just curious . . . did we do something wrong?"*

Before you ask, "Oh my gosh, why would I want to ask such a negative question?" the reason is that there are only two possible responses to the question—a yes or a no. You accept the onus that maybe you did something wrong and set the tone for winning their business back. If they say no, you simply proceed with:

> *"Okay. Well, I would certainly like the opportunity to talk with you about some of the new things we are doing at Creative Training Solutions, and I'd like to set an appointment to discuss them with you in further detail. How does your schedule look on Tuesday at 2:00?"*

If they say yes, they did have a bad experience, proceed with:

"I'm so sorry to hear that! I would like the opportunity to discuss this in further detail and show you how we have changed. How does your schedule look on Tuesday at 2:00?"

Make sure you first apologize, even if you don't feel you did anything wrong. You are genuinely showing empathy and apologizing for the experience. This should disarm them and create an environment in which they will take your suggestion.

Don't get into the details of what went wrong right away. This is still interruptive marketing, and you want the opportunity to do some due diligence on your end. You never want to be treated rudely on the phone, and the elapsed time until the appointment allows for a cool-down. Use the same approach when doing inside sales—setting a phone appointment instead of a physical meeting; you'll get the same benefit during the cool-off period.

FOLLOWING UP WHEN YOU WERE ASKED TO CALL AT A LATER DATE

As we wrote above, the number-one failure of salespeople is lack of follow-through. If you handle your follow-up call after being asked to call back later the way we suggest, you will get the appointment nine times out of ten.

Imagine you ended a call with "How about I call you on [date] and we can set an appointment at that time?" and they said, "Sure." You took great notes and documented the day you promised to call them back. It's now that date and here is Marisa's pattern for what to say:

"Hi John. This is Marisa Pensa with Methods in Motion. We provide customized training programs that have provided impact to the bottom line. The last time we spoke on

[date], you and I agreed I would contact you today to set an appointment. How does your schedule look for Tuesday at 2:00?"

Your prospect will usually remember. If by chance they don't, provide a very brief description of your company and your product or service to help jog their memory. You have done what you promised you would do, you have made a great impression, and you have gained a competitive edge. Keep it simple, and it works!

ACTION STEP

Write down your own roadmaps for upselling or cross-selling an existing customer, reactivating a dormant account, and following up after a set period of time. For the dormant account roadmap be sure to anticipate their saying that you did do something wrong. How will you respond? Practice all these patterns until they sound natural.

CHAPTER 10

CONNECTING WITH THE GRAND POOBAH

"WHAT WOULD I SAY TO THE GRAND POOBAH?"

Now let's dive back into the sales process in general. You're ready to start with HERB—the Highest Executive Responsible for Buying—but perhaps you should go after the Grand Poobah, whom we introduced in chapter 3. If this is a large company, the Grand Poobah could be one or two levels above HERB. You would be leaping to the very top, and you should go for it, especially if you have never done business with this company in the past.

You probably have a lot of questions about this, like "What should I tell the Grand Poobah about my company?" "What kind of voicemail message should I leave if I don't get the Grand Poobah on the phone?" and "What kind of value statement should I have ready to share with the Grand Poobah?" These are all good questions, and we will deal with each of them in later chapters.

For now, though, put these questions aside to make room for this one: "What in the world will I say if I actually get the Grand Poobah on the phone?" Well, what is the purpose of your call? The answer to that question tells you exactly what you need to say to the Grand Poobah on the initial call.

Most salespeople who don't like to call the Grand Poobah actually tried to *sell* to the Grand Poobah on a previous call and it didn't work. As we discussed earlier in regard to calling other players, the purpose of your call is not to close the sale with the Grand Poobah; it's not to schedule a meeting with the Grand Poobah; it's not to get an endorsement from the Grand Poobah; it's not to get any kind of commitment—financial, emotional, or otherwise—from the Grand Poobah. Your purpose is to *get the Grand Poobah's help and guidance.*

Easy enough! Yes, there's a secondary purpose, but if you carry out the primary purpose, the secondary purpose usually takes care of itself. The secondary purpose is to *leave the door open for the Grand Poobah to give you help and guidance in a future call.*

Formulating the opening of this call is pretty simple. It goes like this:

Say hello to the Grand Poobah using their name and identify yourself and your company. For example:

> *"Good morning, Grand Poobah. This is Stacia Skinner from Creative Training Solutions."*

Use both your first and last names when talking to a Grand Poobah. It sounds much more professional than using just your first name. If you're comfortable using your title, go ahead and use it.

Ask directly for help:

> *"I'm hoping you can help me."*

Insert a tiny pause, just long enough to let them interrupt you if they feel like it, but not long enough to be noticeable if they don't. Assuming there is no interruption, briefly explain the kind of help you're looking for. For example:

> *"I'm trying to find the person in charge of your sales training, and I really have nowhere else to turn. I'm hoping you can give me some guidance as to who that would be."*

Wait for the Grand Poobah to respond. Don't go into a long monologue. Stop talking and wait.

How easy is that? Put all your other concerns about voice-mail, your value statement, etc. on hold. Practice this incredibly easy opening, which takes advantage of the fact that the Grand Poobah, probably more than anyone else in the entire organization, *likes* to guide people and tell them what to do. That's what you're going to request on your first call: the Grand Poobah's guidance.

"WHAT WE DO"

At any given moment in your conversation with the Grand Poobah, you must be ready, willing, and able to answer the Grand Poobah's natural and probably inevitable question: "What do you do?" Your response must be phrased somewhat differently from what you've already said about your product or service, and must be concise. Otherwise you run the risk of being perceived as long-winded, rude, or both.

It's probably just as important to understand how *not* to answer the Grand Poobah's question:

- Don't tell your life story, your company's life story, or the life story of your best customer.
- Don't recite a list from your catalog that describes your entire product line.
- Don't read the contents of your brochure or website, or tell them to log on and take a look.

Reply to "What do you do?" by sharing a clear, comprehensible summary of exactly what your company does in terms the Grand Poobah will easily remember ten minutes after the call ends. This statement must take you less than thirty seconds to deliver. It must be totally free of jargon, double-talk, and euphemism. It must give the Grand Poobah the proverbial thirty-thousand-foot view of what you and your organization specialize in. And it must culminate with a restatement of your appeal for their guidance.

Let's look at exactly how this works. Suppose you happen to be in our industry, which is sales training. Here is an example of what your response to the question *should not* sound like:

> "We accelerate sales cycles and critical revenue paths for
> both sales teams and the organizations they serve. We
> do this for a wide range of clients in information-driven
> markets like yours, including several of your counterparts in
> the materials handling and logistics field. Our four primary

modalities for delivering tangible benefits to our clients are: face-to-face behavior modification in on-site prospecting-best-practices sessions; virtual reinforcement of prospecting best practices, delivered both in person and via webinar; and customized interview question development that synchronizes with our Select Plus Senior Level Interviewing model. We've improved cash flow in ninety-eight percent of our client base. Would I talk to you about that, or to someone else?"

That response doesn't precisely tell them what you do. It tells them to bail on your call as soon as humanly possible!

Believe it or not, we really have heard answers like that to the question "What do you do?" Notice how the salesperson artfully maneuvered around the words *sales training*, which are the words the Grand Poobah really needed to hear.

Here's a better response:

"We do sales training."

That short, direct sentence tells them what your call is really about. Notice that it comes first, before any of the following:

"We specialize in helping sales teams like yours improve their company's bottom line."

That's a thirty-thousand-foot view of the benefit you want to present to the Grand Poobah. Notice that it's one sentence long and doesn't contain any fluff or double-talk!

*"The way we accomplish this is to create and deliver tailored
sales training and reinforcement programs for sales teams in
many industries, including [the Grand Poobah's industry]."*

That's another single sentence that relates what you do to the
Grand Poobah's industry. Notice that you're not listing everyone
in their industry your organization has ever worked with, nor
are you reciting your brochure or explaining all of your products
and/or services. Next:

*"I am really hoping you can direct me to the person I should
be talking to about this."*

This is another appeal for help and guidance. Look at it all
again, this time with each of the four elements described:

1. **Short, direct answer to the question:** *"We do sales
   training."*

2. **The benefit, in a single sentence the Grand Poobah
   will understand:** *"We specialize in helping sales teams
   like yours improve their company's bottom line."*

3. **One more one-sentence benefit that references the
   Grand Poobah's industry:** *"The way we accomplish
   this is to create and deliver tailored sales training
   and reinforcement programs for sales teams in many
   industries, including [the Grand Poobah's industry]."*

4. **Ask again for the Grand Poobah's help:** *"I'm really hoping you can direct me to the person I should be talking to about this."*

Before you move on to the next section, write down your own answer to "What do you do?"

WHAT IF THE GRAND POOBAH PUSHES BACK?

One of the most common questions we hear from salespeople who are new to the art of leapfrogging to the Grand Poobah is this one: "How do I handle objections during the prospecting call with the Grand Poobah?" We're actually glad when salespeople ask that, because it allows us to direct the spotlight to one of the biggest reasons to call the Grand Poobah before you call anyone else: *The push-back you get on this kind of call is almost nonexistent.*

A lot of people find this hard to believe, but it really is true. Remember, you're not asking the Grand Poobah for the commitment of a scheduled appointment; you're asking them for guidance. And you're not asking some receptionist, purchasing agent, or mid-level end-user for guidance; you're asking the Grand Poobah. These two facts mean that the vast majority of the "hard" objections you're used to getting during prospecting calls—"We're not interested," "We're all set," etc.—will be replaced by much "softer" responses from the Grand Poobah.

If you do run into a soft but still negative impulsive response from the Grand Poobah, use the same pattern referred to earlier. Here it is:

1. Take down their guard.
2. Repeat their concern.
3. Reassure.
4. Resume.

Below are a variety of responses the Grand Poobah could state and how you would respond:

GRAND POOBAH: *Why would I want [the product or service you sell]?*

Respond with a different *ten-second* benefit statement that concludes with another request for guidance. Here is what it might sound like:

YOU: *I appreciate your asking. Like many in your position, boosting sales can be frustrating and hard to manage. With our proven training methodologies we provide a positive impact that has escalated sales results. That is why I'm trying to find the person in charge of either your sales team or the training of your team. Can you point me in the right direction?*

GRAND POOBAH: *You know what . . . I appreciate your call, but we really don't do that now.*

YOU: *That's okay. In fact, many of my current customers initially told me they weren't doing anything about sales training until we explored the true advantages of what it could do for their bottom line. That's why I'd really like to have the chance to talk to the person who might handle this should the opportunity come up.*

GRAND POOBAH: *I picked the training company we're working with now and we're happy with them.*

YOU: *That's terrific to hear. Actually, many of the companies I work with do have a training company or provide internal training. We find we can be an additional perk to their current programs. I would love the opportunity to show you what we have to offer.*

GRAND POOBAH: *I'm completely swamped right now.*

YOU: *I understand. The only reason I am calling is to ask if you could direct me to the right person to contact regarding sales training.*

And stop talking!

Those are really the toughest objections you're likely to hear on this call. As you can see, they're not really obstacles at all, but opportunities for further conversation in this low-risk, low-commitment, non-confrontational call. The virtual absence of tough objections is one of the reasons we would much rather call on the Grand Poobah than anyone else in the organization. The resistance we get during a typical call is incredibly low!

When the Grand Poobah realizes you are not trying to get an appointment, (unless of course they made the decision to buy whatever it is you have to offer!) but are in fact seeking help and guidance, you will stand out from the crowd, and doors will open for you. If by chance you do have an extended conversation about your product or service with the Grand Poobah, remember to follow these two simple rules:

1. Don't try to sell to the Grand Poobah.
2. Follow the Grand Poobah's lead.

The Grand Poobah will most likely point you toward someone else in the organization. Next you will find out exactly what to do when that happens.

"I HANDLE THAT" OR "TALK TO VALERIE"

You still have the Grand Poobah on the phone. It's very likely that you're wondering what exactly is the agenda for the rest of the discussion. The answer is very simple: The agenda always—repeat, always—is the Grand Poobah's agenda.

Don't try to control the length of the call. Your initial phone conversation with the Grand Poobah could be long or short. It's very likely that the discussion will last sixty seconds or less, but that's entirely up to the Grand Poobah.

Don't try to force-feed the Grand Poobah subjects of your choice during the call. Your initial phone conversation with the Grand Poobah could go into a whole lot of detail about how their organization uses or might use, acquires or might acquire, your product or service. Alternatively, the call might take the proverbial thirty-thousand-foot view. That's entirely up to the Grand Poobah, too.

Remember, you shouldn't try to sell to the Grand Poobah, but it's possible that the Grand Poobah might say, "You know what? I'm the person who handles that. Tell me why we should work with you." In this case, follow their lead, answer all their questions, and leave the question of what happens next entirely up to them, as we did previously. In most cases, however, you will hear something like this:

> *"The person you should be talking to is Valerie, our vice president. She handles that for us. She's at extension 222."*

Hooray! Now you have an internal referral from the Grand Poobah! Valerie is definitely going to treat your call with respect now that the reason for your call is that the Grand Poobah asked you to reach out to her!

THE NEXT STEP IS NON-NEGOTIABLE

Your work with the Grand Poobah is not quite over yet. The moment you hear those words pointing you towards Valerie, or anything close to those words, you must tactfully but purposefully respond with a statement of your own like this:

> *"That's great, Grand Poobah. Thank you so much for pointing me in the right direction. I really appreciate your help! I'll keep you in the loop about what Valerie and I come up with. Could you please transfer me?"*

(It's amazing how many Grand Poobah's don't know how to transfer a call! It's a plus if they do, as the call will be an internal call to Valerie from the Grand Poobah's extension. How likely is it that Valerie will pick up that call? Pretty darn likely!)

Thank the Grand Poobah and tell them *tactfully* that you will be keeping them in the loop. Notice that you don't *ask* the Grand Poobah whether or not it's okay to keep them in the loop. This is simply how you do business: you keep them in the loop, via phone, snail mail, email, or whichever way makes the most sense.

We suggest keeping the Grand Poobah in the loop with a handwritten note. After you have spoken to and met with Valerie, write the Grand Poobah a personal note and thank them again for the referral and keep them abreast of what you are talking with Valerie about. You started with the Grand Poobah and you don't want to lose that connection.

So far we've looked at what you should do if you manage to reach the Grand Poobah voice-to-voice. But what should you do if the Grand Poobah doesn't pick up? In the next chapter we cover how to leave the perfect voicemail message for the Grand Poobah. It's a lot easier than you might think!

ACTION STEPS

Think of five companies you would like to sell to that you're not currently selling to—companies that you **have not** called before. Invest some time online identifying the Grand Poobah at all five of these companies. The Grand Poobah is one or two levels higher than HERB.

Write down your "what I do" statement. When the Grand Poobah asks, "What do you do?" how will you address number one below? Then write your roadmap for numbers 2 through 4 below.

1. Short, direct answer to the question

2. The benefit, in a single sentence the Grand Poobah will understand

3. One more one-sentence benefit that references the Grand Poobah's industry

4. Ask again for the Grand Poobah's help

KEEPING THE GRAND POOBAH IN THE LOOP

"HOW DO I KEEP THE GRAND POOBAH IN THE LOOP?"

If you follow all the strategies you've learned so far in *Competitive Selling*, again you will:

- Start your sales cycle higher in the organization.
- Generate more quality conversations with the Grand Poobah.
- Generate more quality appointments with HERB.
- Secure more high-quality referrals from the Grand Poobah
- Accelerate your sales cycle.

Believe it! That's what happens if you practice and execute everything we've shared with you to this point. And if you follow the advice in this chapter, you'll also enjoy a benefit that most salespeople would do just about anything to secure: close bigger-than-average deals, thanks to the Grand Poobah's ability to instantly expand relationships with any and all favored suppliers.

How do you pull this off? By keeping the Grand Poobah in the loop throughout the entire sales cycle! This is actually far easier to do than you might imagine. Let's assume you had a good conversation with the Grand Poobah and that they pointed you toward Sam or HERB. You call this person, mention that the Grand Poobah suggested you get in touch, and, using the strategies from earlier in the book, set up a date and time for your first substantial discussion. This discussion can take the form of a face-to-face meeting or a scheduled phone conversation.

The minute you complete your first substantial conversation with Sam or HERB, send a *handwritten, hand-addressed, hand-stamped* note to the Grand Poobah updating them regarding your meeting. If you keep it short, sweet, and to the point, this correspondence will definitely aid your cause. The note you send should read something like this:

> *Dear Grand Poobah,*
>
> *Thank you for the referral to [name] regarding sales training. [Name] and I met yesterday, and we had a great conversation regarding your training initiatives. We are meeting again on December 15th at 2:00 to further our discussion. I hope we have the pleasure of meeting in the future. Thank you again.*
>
> *Best regards,*
> *Stacia Skinner*

Remember, this is a *handwritten, hand-addressed, hand-stamped* correspondence. If you take the time to write it, the Grand Poobah will take the time to read it. And yes, the Grand Poobah will be the person who opens and reads this message. Make sure you also include your business card with the note so they have your information. The more personal it looks, the less likely their assistant is to open it!

You can follow a similar procedure if the Grand Poobah's assistant gives you a referral. Just thank them and keep them in the loop about when and where your next meeting is scheduled. And don't be surprised if the Grand Poobah shows up for the meeting!

LEAVING A VOICEMAIL MESSAGE FOR THE GRAND POOBAH

To this point the focus has been on what to say and how to respond if you reach the Grand Poobah directly, voice-to-voice. That's obviously an important scenario for you to prepare for, but you are more likely to reach the Grand Poobah's voicemail than you are to reach them voice-to-voice. First let's look at three things you definitely *do not* want to do:

1. **Don't hang up and not leave a message at all.**
   Although few, if any, managers, trainers, and senior salespeople advocate doing this, we believe the majority of salespeople who call the Grand Poobah and don't get them on the line bail out on the call when they reach voicemail. They do this because they're not sure what to say. That's too bad, because the numbers definitely favor those who leave the right kind of message via voicemail.

2. **Don't launch into a huge speech about anything, including something you plan to send or have already sent the Grand Poobah.** Yes, there are a lot of selling programs out there that tell you to leave an intricate, carefully scripted message about what's coming, what's already arrived, or what you're thinking of sending. Most of these programs ask you to develop a power statement to capture the Grand Poobah's attention at the very beginning of the voicemail message. Our experience is that long messages simply don't work. We suspect that in most cases the Grand Poobah (or their assistant) simply deletes these messages. Don't share success stories. Don't show off all your research.

3. **Don't use voicemail to request the Grand Poobah's help in identifying HERB.** Save this for your voice-to-voice conversation. Sharing this level of detail in your voicemail message takes away the advantage of piquing their curiosity.

Leave a very simple message that sounds something like this:

"Grand Poobah, this is Marisa Pensa from Methods in Motion. I am really hoping you can help me. Please call me at 555-555-5555. I would appreciate it. Again, this is Marisa Pensa 555-555-5555. Thank you."

You can vary the wording, but don't vary the basic structure. The idea is to deliver a brief, hard-to-delete request for help that piques the Grand Poobah's curiosity. Here's a perfectly good variation:

> *"Hi Grand Poobah. This is Stacia Skinner from Creative Training Solutions. My number is 555-555-5555. I'm calling because I'm looking for your guidance and direction. Can you please give me a call? My number again is 555-555-5555. Thanks so much."*

Or you might simply leave this message:

> *"Hello, Grand Poobah. This is Stacia Skinner from Creative Training Solutions. I am hoping you can help me. If you could call me back, my number is 555-555-5555. Again Stacia Skinner, my number is 555-555-5555. Thank you."*

It's that simple. Make the words your own, but whatever you do, don't make the message more complicated than the examples here!

When you get a return call, ask for help. Most people—and certainly most Grand Poobahs—speak very, very fast during the first few seconds of the call, like this:

> *"HiyaitsPoobahJonesyoucalledmewhatcanIdoforyou?"*

Did you actually catch their name or where they are from? Probably not. They just did interruptive marketing to you. You were not waiting with bated breath looking for your phone to ring. You were doing something else and when the phone rang it interrupted what you were doing.

Feel free to say:

> *"Grand Poobah—Thank you so much for returning my call. I definitely recognize I called you and would like to*

reference the research I did prior to calling. Would you please remind me what company you're calling from?"

Or, if you did not catch their name and company:

"Thank you so much for the return call. I am so sorry but I did not catch your name and what company you are calling from. Could you repeat that for me?"

Nine times out of ten they will be happy to explain where they're calling from and you'll have a moment to catch your breath and get your bearings. You can then use the customized approach you developed earlier.

ACTION STEPS

1. Create and practice a simple voicemail message. Then call your own voicemail and leave yourself a message using your message. Listen to and critique your message. Finally, play your best message for a trusted friend or colleague and ask for feedback.

2. Using the principles you have learned thus far, call five Grand Poobahs. Warm up by role-playing and practicing first! Be ready to leave your voicemail message if you don't reach them.

3. If you reach a prospect through a referral, make sure to write a thank-you note after your first meeting to the Grand Poobah.

CHAPTER 12

SAYING HELLO TO SAM, HERB'S ASSISTANT

I run into a lot of salespeople who are looking for a reason—any reason—*not* to leapfrog a Gatekeeper to HERB or the Grand Poobah. It's not that they don't like calling HERB or the Grand Poobah; what they really don't like is going outside their comfort zone. One of the most common excuses we get sounds something like this: "Why even bother trying to reach out to HERB or the Grand Poobah? My call is just going to get screened by a Gatekeeper." This is really not a good excuse because, lucky for you, you will be screened—although we prefer the word *met*—not just by the Gatekeeper, but by HERB's assistant or the Grand Poobah's assistant, Sam. And Sam is, or at least can be, your good friend.

The first voice you will hear when calling a company is the general receptionist, who in most cases is *not* Sam. Remember, Sam is HERB's assistant, and they may also be your biggest asset when it comes to making inroads in HERB's organization.

Sam is HERB's or the Grand Poobah's right hand, eyes, and ears. Not only that, Sam is almost certainly the person who is listening to *all* the voicemail messages you leave for HERB or the Grand Poobah. One of the reasons we urge salespeople to leave multiple—polite!—voicemail messages is that Sam is likely to audition salespeople by evaluating the quality, tact, and persistence of their messages for HERB or the Grand Poobah. None of this makes Sam an obstacle to your sales process, though. In fact, Sam can be, and should be, your most important *ally* in the sales process!

Sam is not an extension of the front desk person who fields your calls. To the contrary, Sam is an extension of HERB and the Grand Poobah! That means Sam deserves to be treated with the same respect as HERB and the Grand Poobah, not just because HERB and the Grand Poobah usually empower Sam to make decisions about who talks to whom, but also because Sam knows more than anyone in the organization besides HERB and the Grand Poobah about the business you want to do with them. (And let's be brutally honest here—some Sams actually know a good deal more about what's actually going on in the organization than some tunnel-visioned HERBs and Grand Poobahs do.)

WHAT TO SAY TO SAM

Let's look now at how to talk to Sam if they happen to answer the phone. It should come as no surprise to learn that the song you should be hearing in your head during each and every interaction with Sam is the old Aretha Franklin hit, "Respect." If Sam gets undeniable R-E-S-P-E-C-T from you over the phone, your relationship with them will be fine and you will make forward progress on your sales process (which is, of course, what you're after).

On the other hand, if Sam ever gets the sense that you're copping an attitude with them, or treating them as a minor functionary, or blowing off steam in their direction, you will be Dead with a capital "D" for the foreseeable future at Sam's organization. You can get back in the door but it might involve groveling and apologizing. Obviously you don't ever want to go down that road if you can help it.

Speak just as confidently and purposefully with Sam as you do with HERB and the Grand Poobah. Don't fall prey to the Winnie-the-Pooh Syndrome here either! If your voice sounds professional and goal-oriented, you'll do fine with Sam. If you sound wishy-washy, you'll quickly find Sam has no time for you.

Here is a best practice we learned from dealing with hundreds of Sams over the years, a tactic that can get Sam on your side almost instantly. It is incredibly effective at breaking down barriers and building rapport with Sam if you use it at the right time, which is within the first two or three seconds of the call. If you miss that very first window, however, it's not much use to you later. When Sam answers the phone, you will usually hear the following habit-driven, only-semi-conscious opening:

> *"HERB's [or The Grand Poobah's] office. This is Sam. How can I help you?"*

When you hear these words, or any variation on them, do *not* launch into any attempt to get Sam to help you. Instead, smile and enthusiastically say something like this:

> *"Oh, Sam, I'm* really *hoping you can!"*

Then stop talking.

When you do this, something truly amazing happens. No matter how busy they are, no matter how their day is going, no matter what else is going on in the organization, Sam will lighten up. They will chuckle. They will laugh. They will even say something like "I'll certainly give it my best shot!" We can't tell you what a big difference this positive response can make in the outcome of your call!

This opening might seem like a minor strategy, but it's not. It can have a huge impact on having a good, productive call with Sam. We use this approach as often as possible in our initial calls to Sam. You should, too!

GETTING HELP FROM SAM: TWO PATHS

Now you can politely and respectfully tell Sam what they can help you with. There are two possible paths here.

PATH ONE: If you're calling a small company where you know HERB probably has direct input into purchase decisions related to what you sell, your goal is to ask Sam for help and guidance in connecting you with HERB. The structure and tone of this request are very similar to the request you make to the Grand Poobah when you ask for their guidance and assistance. The difference is you're appealing to Sam as the expert when it comes to reaching HERB. What you say on path one might sound like this:

> *"Sam, this is Marisa Pensa from Methods in Motion . I'm trying to reach HERB. [Or I've been trying to reach HERB for a while.] Do you know the best way for me to contact [him/her]?"*

Or:

"Sam, my name is Stacia Skinner from Creative Training Solutions. We provide sales training, and I'm trying to reach HERB. Can you guide me as to the best way I can get a hold of [him/her]?"

Or:

"Sam, my name is Marisa Pensa from Methods in Motion. We provide sales training, and I've been trying to reach HERB. By any chance do you hold [his/her] calendar?"

It's amazing how many Sams will actually state they do and will put you in HERB's calendar. Remember that you're not issuing orders or instructions to Sam, nor are you demanding updates about whether messages have been received or acted upon. Just as in the situation in which you reached HERB voice-to-voice, you are asking Sam for help and guidance—and treating them as a trusted advisor!

Follow Sam's lead! Listen carefully to what they tell you about the best way to connect with HERB or the Grand Poobah!

PATH TWO: If you're calling a large company where you think HERB probably doesn't have direct input into purchase decisions related to what you sell, ask Sam for help and guidance in connecting with the person who handles what you sell.

If you are pretty certain that the Grand Poobah doesn't inspect individual invoices or talk to individual vendors who sell stuff like yours, you don't need to reach the Grand Poobah; you want Sam's help and guidance in connecting you with the right

HERB. If you're calling a Fortune 500 or 1000 company, or a company of comparable size and complexity, path two is the one we recommend.

On path two, summarize exactly what you do, but use even more concise wording than you would for HERB. Then immediately ask Sam to point you in the right direction in their organization. What you say might sound like this:

> "Sam, this is Stacia Skinner from Creative Training Solutions. We're a sales training company and I need to connect with the person who handles sales training for your company. Do you have any idea who that might be?"

Or:

> "Sam, my name is Marisa Pensa from Methods in Motion. We are a sales training company. I've been tossed around your company for a bit, and I'm just hoping you can direct me to the best person who is in charge of your sales training."

Notice that you *should not* deliver the same detailed value statement to Sam that you would deliver to HERB. Keep it short and sweet. Sam is busy! You want to get direction and guidance from Sam *and* make their life easier so they can go on to the next thing on their to-do list.

Follow Sam's lead! Listen to what they tell you about the person you should talk to next.

DEALING WITH PUSH-BACK FROM SAM

In very rare cases Sam will push back, but it's likely to be low in intensity and fairly easy to address. At a small company (path one), Sam's push-back is likely to sound like this:

> "HERB's awfully hard to reach [this week/this month/this quarter]."

Your response to this is quite simple:

> "That's okay, Sam. I completely understand. Would it make more sense for me to call back [next week/month/quarter]?"

Your goal here is to set up another point of contact *without challenging or contradicting Sam in any way.*

At a large company (path two), Sam's push-back is likely to sound like this:

> "Tell me more about what you do."

They're asking this in order to figure out the right person to send you to. If—*and only if*—you hear this response, you will know Sam has time to listen to a short summary of what you do. Your response is to walk Sam through the same concise value statement you would have shared with HERB, and wait to see where Sam points you.

Don't challenge, belittle, or try to wiggle around a referral from Sam. Simply thank them for their help and call the referral they recommend.

When you interact with Sam—via voicemail, phone, email, or any other form of contact—keep all your communications exquisitely polite and respectful. Your good relationship with Sam is like a permanent "Get Out of Jail Free" card in a game of Monopoly. It's incredibly valuable. But the minute you tick Sam off you'll find you can no longer use the card!

ACTION STEPS

1. Go through your list of five companies you developed in the Action Step in chapter 10. Are there any at which you already know Sam's name and/or have a relationship with them? Write them down and ask yourself whether Sam can help you.

2. Practice speaking with Sam with a friend or colleague. Then call one of the companies on your list with the goal of reaching either HERB or Sam. Decide ahead of time whether you will follow path one or path two if you happen to reach Sam. Be sure to practice and do some role-playing with a real, live person before you get on the phone!

CHAPTER 13

YOU GOT THE REFERRAL. NOW WHAT?

You've gotten HERB or the Grand Poobah (or, in a large organization, Sam) to point you toward the person in the organization you should be talking to—the Decision Influencer. Now what do you do? You try to leverage this referral into a scheduled discussion with them. This might be a VP, a manager, or any number of administrators. Say something like this:

"Good morning, Decision Influencer. This is Stacia Skinner from Creative Training Solutions. We provide customized training programs designed to provide impact to your bottom line. Did the office of [HERB, or the Grand Poobah] tell you I was going to call? [Wait for their response.] [She/He] told me you were the right person to talk to regarding training, and suggested we should talk. I would like to set an appointment with you. How about this Tuesday at 2:00?"

Yes, you really do need to ask for the appointment this directly and this immediately. You have to assume that when either HERB, the Grand Poobah, or Sam pointed you toward this person, there was a reason. So follow through and ask them directly for the meeting. Sometimes the recommendation doesn't lead you to the right person, but more often than not, it does. *Respect Sam's or HERB's and the Grand Poobah's recommendation and go from there.*

Your goal is *to set a face-to-face appointment* (or, if you sell over the phone, win a scheduled time for an initial call) with the Decision Influencer. You are not trying to sell during this initial call. In fact, you're not even trying to have any kind of detailed conversation. The less said during this initial exchange, the better! (Inside sales professionals: please refer to chapter 8 for more on this.)

There are a lot of ways this scenario can play out. Let's look at some of them now. As soon as possible after you get the referral from HERB's office, reach out by phone to the person you've been referred to. The most likely outcome, of course, is that you're going to leave a brief voicemail message. The first half of the message should sound like this:

> *"Hello, Decision Influencer. This is Marisa Pensa from Methods in Motion. My number is 555-555-5555. I'm calling regarding HERB [or the Grand Poobah.]"*

Once again, notice what you *don't* say. Don't say, "HERB [or the Grand Poobah] told me to call." Don't say, "HERB said you're the best thing since sliced bread." Don't say, "The Grand Poobah said I'm supposed to meet with you." This has to be a concise, direct message that prompts an instant returned call. The word *regarding* is very important. It piques the question, "Regarding what?" Notice the difference in the wording of these two messages.

Don't say:

> *"Hello, Decision Influencer. This is Marisa Pensa from Methods in Motion. HERB [or the Grand Poobah] suggested that I contact you and I would love the opportunity to get together with you. Please call me at 555-555-5555. I am really looking forward to your call."*

Do say:

> *"Hello, Decision Influencer. This is Stacia Skinner from Creative Training Solutions. I'm calling regarding HERB [or the Grand Poobah]. Again, my name is Stacia Skinner; my number is 555-555-5555."*

Here's the second half of the message:

> *"Again, my name is Stacia Skinner and my number is 555-555-5555. Thank you."*

Yes, it really should be that short! Leave this message and see what happens.

If HERB or the Grand Poobah referred you, the game plan for what to say when you reach the Decision Influencer is almost as simple as when you reached HERB or the Grand Poobah. First build up a little rapport, introduce yourself, and share the same short benefit statement you shared with HERB or the Grand

Poobah. That will take maybe five seconds. Then—remembering that you will not interview, fact-find, or probe during this call—attempt to close on the appointment. After the call opening, in which you give your name and your company name in the same way as the previous examples, say something like this:

> *"Did HERB [or the Grand Poobah] tell you I was going to give you a call?"*

Let the Decision Influencer respond. In most cases the answer will be no. That's fine. It allows you to transition seamlessly into the request for the appointment, which sounds like this:

> *"Well, HERB [or the Grand Poobah] told me you were the right person to contact about [sales training/ widgets/whatever] and suggested we [get together/talk]."*

Don't be afraid to use these words. When HERB or the Grand Poobah told you to call the Decision Influencer, they were suggesting that you connect. You should tell the Decision Influencer this. Continue with:

> *"I'd like to set an appointment with you. How's this Tuesday at 2:00?"*

Notice that you ask directly for the appointment by specifying the exact time and date you want for the meeting. Posing the question this way means that the most likely negative response will be "Well, Tuesday at 2:00 doesn't work for me." You can then suggest another date: "How's Wednesday at 3:00?"

Remember, your first, last, and only goal in this discussion is to set the initial appointment!

If you received the referral from Sam, address the Decision Influencer slightly differently. It might sound something like this:

> *"Hi Decision Influencer. This is Marisa Pensa from Methods in Motion. Did HERB's **office** tell you I would be giving you a call? [Pause for a response.] They told me you were the right person to contact regarding sales training and suggested we should get together. I would like to set an appointment with you. How's Tuesday at 2:00?"*

If you did not talk directly to HERB or the Grand Poobah, but talked to Sam, don't say you talked to *them!* This will backfire. Make sure you ask, "Did HERB's **office** tell you I was going to call?" This is very important.

Again, no matter whether the referral you get is from HERB or from Sam, your first, last, and only goal in this discussion is to set the initial appointment!

ACTION STEPS

Using the principles you have learned to this point, call the referrals you have gained. Leave voicemail messages as suggested and see what happens.

CHAPTER 14

YOU'VE GOT MAIL— VOICEMAIL AND EMAIL

Marisa's story: "I never used to leave voicemail messages. My mindset was always to just call back at another time. No one would out-work me and I would eventually reach my prospect. As time went on I had less and less time to prospect. The precious hours available for making prospecting calls forced me to get more creative and take a hard look at how to make the most of limited selling time.

"The general consensus about voicemail is 'No one ever calls back.' And I used to be on that same bandwagon. I remember telling a mentor of mine about my belief that voicemails didn't work. He asked me, 'Marisa, is that just your theory or have you spent thirty years seeing clients get return calls from messages?' My response was, 'Well, if you say it that way, I guess it's just my theory.'

"The 'no one calls back' consensus is true to some extent, and more true now than in past years, but this could be because you quit after leaving one voicemail that doesn't get a response. In this case you should have low expectations for returned calls. However,

if you follow our formula for mixing voicemail and email together, and plan the right timing between each touch, you will get a great result.

"Some of my best appointments have come on the fourth or fifth touch, and both the satisfied customers and I are grateful that I didn't give up before that point.

"One example of persistence paying off is a company that has been a customer of mine for the past eight years. In about the seventh year things had gone stagnant. One manager gave me a nudge to call Julie, the new director of training. I thought this warm call would be easy; I had permission to use the manager's name and the company was already a customer of mine. This was not a cold call but it took me two voicemails, an email, and then another voicemail to make it through to Julie and set an appointment.

"During our lunch appointment Julie profusely apologized for being so hard to reach. She thanked me for sticking with it and said she did want to meet but had been so buried she just couldn't see straight. This encouraged me to stick with it with other prospects. Yes, there is a point at which you should stop calling and just let it rest, but too often we give up way too quickly."

A LOOK AT VOICEMAIL

Always pick up the phone first and never default to email as your first approach. It's far too easy to just delete an email, and it doesn't give you a competitive edge. Some prospects don't return voicemail because the salesperson spoke too fast and the message or the return phone number wasn't clear. But the reality is that most voicemails don't get returned because they sound like sales calls!

In Marisa's story above, Julie knew who Marisa was and about her company. She actually wanted to meet, but was just so buried she never responded. Like many others she had so much on her plate that even someone she wanted to meet with went to the bottom of the priorities she was juggling. Stay the course and it will pay off.

Realize every time you leave a voicemail your prospect is hearing your voice, which is not a bad thing! Every time they hear you, this in turn is the start of building a business relationship. Business is still built on one old school principle: Relationships! Even in today's technology-driven world, relationships are still important to the buyer, and they are grown through face-to-face or voice-to-voice dialog. Never look at leaving a voicemail as a waste of time because it's not! Even though you feel it is a one-way street, it is the very beginning of building that relationship, which is what we all strive to achieve with our customers.

So how do you guard against your calls sounding like sales calls? Leave a message with intrigue that piques their curiosity. Here's the pattern for leaving any message:

1. Your name
2. Company name
3. Phone number
4. Calling in reference to . . .
5. Your name
6. Phone number
7. Thank you

Notice that at the end you just say "Thank you" rather than "Looking forward to your call" or "Have a great day." A simple thank you makes the message more intriguing. Sales calls typically end with "Looking forward to your call" or some other type of hugs and kisses. "Thank you" doesn't alert the person that this is a sales call. It might be something else.

For the "calling in reference to . . . ," aim for one word or one phrase, but keep it short and concise. Here are some examples:

- A client name in a vertical market
- The name of a specific product you know they use
- A specific event
- The name of the referral source
- The date you last called
- Or "I was specifically pointed in your direction."

Notice that "I was pointed in your direction *regarding sales training* [or your industry]" is *not* in the list. Avoid overexplaining that line to make it sound less like a sales call and bring more intrigue to the person receiving it.

If you refer to a client in a vertical market, avoid mentioning "the work we've done with XYZ company in your industry," which makes it sound like a sales call.

Trust us. This formula will get your phone ringing! Everything new feels uncomfortable at first. Try wearing your watch on the opposite wrist for even one hour and you'll want to change it back! You're just doing something different, so stick with it long enough to experience the results.

Here are some guidelines to consider when leaving voicemail:

1. Do not expect to get a call back when you leave voicemail. If you do, view it as a gift.

2. When you get on the phone, expect the person you are calling to answer so you are prepared verses expecting to get voicemail.

3. Less said the better. Give them a reason to call you back.

4. When stating your phone number, *slow down!* Write it in the air while you are saying it. If you can't write it, neither can they. Also, if there is a zero in your number, say the word "zero," not "O," because you cannot hear "O" on voicemail.

5. Always state your name and number twice so the person you are calling does not have to go back into your voicemail.

6. When leaving the "regarding" on the first two voicemails, be short, direct, and limit your wording.

7. After leaving two or three voicemails, email your contact to gain a response.

Now let's consider the frequency of calling and what happens when you don't get a call back. You are going to leave two voicemails with the same message in six days. Your next message (and you're not going to email just yet) should be about three business days later. We love this voicemail and it results in even more callbacks than your first two. But you have to have left at least one voicemail to have a shot at getting a callback from this one. It goes like this:

1. Your name
2. Company name
3. Phone number

4. "I left you a message last week and am so sorry we never connected!"
5. Your name
6. Phone number
7. Thank you

It's not necessary to restate the reference line. Just keep it short and sweet.

After another three days with no return call, it's time to email. You have attempted to reach your contact two or three times by phone and they have heard your voice and the effort you've put in. There is something about the sound of a person's voice that cuts through the noise and forms a connection, as we mentioned above. Each time they hear your voice, you are building a relationship.

Most emails do get deleted when they are not solicited, but the one you will send is different. People open an email because of the subject line and who it comes from. They respond to the email because of the content. Here is an example of the email you will send:

Subject: *Tried Unsuccessfully to Reach [or Contact] You*

Hi John,

In recent days I have tried to reach you by phone and thought email might be an easier way for us to connect.

My intention for reaching out is to schedule an appointment with you. I would like to share some observations and trends we have seen in your industry and how we have helped provide a positive impact on the bottom line.

How does your schedule look for us to get together at one of the times below?

Option 1: [Date/time]

Option 2: [Date/time]

Option 3: [Date/time]

If these are not convenient, please let me know if there are a couple other alternative dates that would be better for your schedule.

Thank you.

[Your signature]

Notice the subject line. You are making it clear that you have attempted to communicate with them before. People do open this email. This subject line works in our business and across other industries.

For accounts that are worth it, you might prospect for a year or more to get in the door. But not through nonstop weekly calling. If you have a contact's number on your speed-dial and they haven't picked up your call for months, *stop calling!* You're being a pest. There's a fine line between being a pest and being persistent. If they haven't contacted you after seven touches, put it on the back burner and revisit it at a later time.

If your contact hasn't responded to your email within five days, leave a voicemail something like this one:

"Hi John. This is Marisa Pensa with Methods in Motion. I'm so sorry I missed you a couple of times and I assume this is probably just really bad timing for you. I definitely don't want to pester you! If you've been meaning to call me, please reach out to me at [say number twice]; otherwise I'll plan to contact you again on [a date that's two months later]. Thank you!"

This voicemail does not mean you're giving up. It just means the timing is not right. Sales is about timing. If someone has not responded to you after five to seven touches it might not be the right timing. But don't give up too soon. Just let it rest for a while after the above voicemail and go back to it at a later date.

ACTION STEP

Call yourself and practice leaving the voicemail that you would leave for a potential client. Then call a colleague and leave one. Ask your colleague to critique your message. Would you or your colleague call you back?

Come up with a variety of "regardings" you can use to gain the curiosity of the person you are calling.

Keep track of when you are leaving voicemails. Don't let more than three days go by before leaving another touchpoint via voicemail or email.

CHAPTER 15

VOCAL CONTROL AND TONE

Y*our authentic, enthusiastic, positive vocal tone is the key to making all of this work!*

This prospecting system relies heavily on phone contact, which means it relies heavily on the right vocal presentation. The right vocal tone quickly conveys the right person-to-person attitude over the phone . . . and the right attitude means everything. It can rescue you from the most disastrous mistake on the phone; it can allow you to establish a solid, positive, authentic initial connection with HERB, the Grand Poobah, and Sam, or anyone else in the organization. On the other hand, the *wrong* vocal tone, or the *wrong* attitude, can sabotage any call, even one in which you are carefully following all the rules we've laid out for you in the previous chapters!

The right tone gives you the right to start over, regardless of any error in execution you may make along the way. No matter how "bad" your first call is, if your tone is confident and curious and engaging, you can create a connection and generate a chuckle here and there so you can enjoy each other's company over the phone. You will have established a bond that you can leverage in a lot of different ways.

Remember, you're building relationships more than anything else, and your call is the start of a relationship. It's a first impression, and first impressions can make you or break you.

Making a good first impression over the phone is hard, though, because you and the other person don't have the benefit of seeing each other face to face. Professor Albert Mehrabian did a lot of research into how human beings assimilate information. He concluded that 55 percent of the information we take in is visual, 7 percent is in the wording, and 38 percent is in the vocal delivery. That means that 55 percent of any conversation depends on things like body language, eye contact, and facial expressions, and you have none of that on the phone! All you have is your voice, so you have to be sure to use that tool to send the right message.

Not only that, if the other person has completely tuned out of the conversation and started doodling, playing a game, or texting someone, you have no way of knowing! Dr. Mehrabian also concluded that people interpret your message on the phone based on the tone of your voice rather than on the words you choose—86 percent of the time.

Here's the bottom line: You will live or die on these calls based on your ability to use your vocal delivery to command and hold attention. Here are five simple things you can do to improve your vocal tone on the phone:

1. **Breathe deeply.** Your voice is the product of the air you take into and let out of your body. Shallow breathing

means a shallow, halting delivery. Get your lungs full of air!

2. **Lubricate your voice.** Drink eight ounces of water every hour. Caffeinated beverages like soda, tea, and coffee don't count, and actually do more harm than good. Caffeine dehydrates your vocal components and makes you sound worse.

3. **Smile.** Believe it or not, your vocal delivery will improve if you put a mirror up near your desk and check it regularly to make sure you're smiling (instead of grimacing) as you make your calls. You can also place a photo that makes you smile where you will see it when you're on the phone. Everyone has heard the phrase: "Smile and Dial." It works!

4. **Use plenty of gestures when you make your calls.** Even though the other person can't see them, they help you sound more purposeful, positive, and believable. You know when you get excited your voice tone goes up, and you might sit straighter in your chair or even stand up. I can guarantee that your arms start flailing and your hands make gestures too. People can hear that on the phone.

5. **Analyze your calls.** Record your half of the conversation and play it back. Listen critically to what you hear. Do you sound authentic or fake? Do you sound relaxed or stressed? Would you refer yourself?

Would you set up an appointment with yourself? Be your own worst critic!

Eighty percent of the sale is *you*. You want them to like you. You are selling an appointment with you when you are on the phone. People love to do business with people who love what they do. Convey that you love what you do with a positive tone and vocal control to bring out the best in you.

There are times when your head gets in your way. You become a "Debbie Downer" because you had a bad call or something bad happened or you're in a sales slump—you're riding the negative train. Don't get on the phone when you feel like this because people can hear it. Take a step back and focus on the positives of what your prospecting call can do for you!

Instead of dreading the call and thinking of the negatives that can happen when you are making this initial contact, reset your mind and think about the positives that can come out of making the call. Just before you are about to dial, take a moment to reflect, and think of the following questions and the answers you might receive to get yourself in a positive state of mind:

- What are the positives that could come out of this call?
- Could this call be the start of a relationship that will give me a brand new client?
- Could this call help me hit or exceed my goals?
- Could this call bring me a great commission check?

Just reading these questions gives you a positive feeling and puts you in a better state of mind to make the call. Think of the positives and you will see how easy these calls can be!

ACTION STEP

If your calls are not already being recorded at your office, use the voice memo on your cell phone and record your side of the conversation for one phone call. Then listen to it and critique yourself. What rating would you give yourself on your level of enthusiasm and passion? (Use a scale of 1 to 5 with 5 being the highest.)

CHAPTER 16

PUTTING IT ALL TOGETHER—THE MULTIPLE TOUCH RULE

N ow that you've learned the broad outline of this prospecting system, you should master two critical principles to successfully implement these ideas. They are fairly simple principles that greatly enhance your odds of success, but we find that a lot of the salespeople we work with overlook them when they start to work with our patterns.

IMPLEMENTATION PRINCIPLE #1: *Real learning means doing, and doing means practice.*

Just reading about this prospecting system is not enough. If you expect it to work for you, you need to carefully review the ideas, principles, and strategies we have shared in a way that feels natural to you, and you need to practice them. That's how human beings learn—not just by reading a book, but by taking action—by practicing and doing.

We are active learners. If we don't eventually take some kind of action involving what we're learning, we don't really learn. It took us over two decades of active trial and error to get this system to the point where it works consistently for us. It would be a big mistake for you to expect to get the same results from a day or two of haphazard calling. So practice . . . and give yourself some time to learn. Three to six weeks of sustained effort and practice, for at least fifteen minutes a day, is a good target once you've finished reading *Competitive Selling*.

IMPLEMENTATION PRINCIPLE #2: *Don't practice on HERB.*

We are always amazed by salespeople who hear our prospecting system, get all excited, and run off to start their day with a rusty, amateurish, unprepared call to a real live prospect. Even if you're confident you have the whole system down (and let's face it, at this stage you probably don't), how about a few minutes of warm-up role-playing with a colleague or even a one-sided call that you record and review by yourself *before* you dial your prospect? A conversation with any of these players is a precious opportunity, and you don't want to be surprised by an unexpected response and waste that opportunity. After all, there are only so many prospects in your territory!

This system is first and foremost a reliable method for leaving a good first impression with these players by phone. It works . . . *if* you put in the practice ahead of time—like an Olympic-level skater preparing for a gold-medal performance. Leaving a good first impression is like delivering a great routine on the ice; the performance looks effortless and graceful from a distance if you put in the time, effort, and energy necessary to master your routine. But if you stumble out there with little or no preparation time, or without being "in the zone," you will fall on your keister and get low marks from the judges.

For example, we trained a salesperson in this system and he just dove right in. We told him it was too soon to try live calls, but he had been running his own business for a long time and was positive that he'd be fine.

His ratios weren't good at all: forty-two dials resulting in seven contacts and no appointments. We asked him, "What in the world are you doing?" Once we role-played with him we saw that he hadn't been putting anything into practicing what we had taught him, and had been running with his old habits. He came off sounding like an amateur. If potential clients sense that you're an amateur, they'll eat you alive.

You know who's really good at spotting amateurs? HERB— along with the Grand Poobah. And so is Sam. Sam can sniff out amateurs in a second. HERB is definitely worth a gold-medal performance; and don't forget about the Grand Poohbah and the other players who could be involved. So get yourself "in the zone" by giving yourself a little practice time with a colleague, a recorder, or both before you step out in front of the judges.

CHAPTER 17

THE COMPETITIVE SELLING ADVANTAGE

As we mentioned in the beginning of the book, there's a big difference between pitch selling, consultative selling, and competitive selling. The big advantage of competitive selling is gained by going after the HERBs and the Grand Poobahs. Competitive sellers focus on performance under pressure and being the best they can be against their competition.

We're talking about doing something different from what everyone else in your market is doing. Gain the competitive edge by going to the top of an organization or department instead of going where it's easy to get someone on the phone, which is usually at the bottom.

Let's say you're biking to the top of a mountain. It's strenuous. It takes a ton of energy, focus, balance, and time. Once you've climbed to the top and started going down the other side, you have momentum behind you. It doesn't take nearly as long, the ride is fun, and it requires a whole lot less energy.

Now think about the tendency to start at the bottom in the sales process. It's very easy to get people at the lower levels to talk to you, but that's not where HERB is. You have to go higher up. To get there it does take longer, and more effort is needed, but the reward is greater. Your sales process will go a lot more smoothly, just like riding down the mountain.

Is it frustrating trying to get to HERB or the Grand Poobah? Yes, it is. Will you always get there? No, you won't. But the rewards you receive for going from the top down come faster, and they are often more profitable than going from the bottom up. This is the competitive advantage—and how you gain the edge over your competition.

Stacia's story: "Let me share two stories related to reaching out to HERB. The first is about a slam-dunk as a result of going high in an organization. I decided to call on a major hotel chain. I had nothing to lose so I decided to call the VP of sales. It took me over a month to reach him, but once I did I set the appointment. Within two months of that meeting I was doing my first training program. That was a fast sales process in my business. He was definitely the '51-percenter,' and it worked.

"The second is about a long, drawn-out slugfest of a sales process. I met a prospect at a trade show and thought this person was HERB. I called and set an appointment, and our conversations dragged out for over a year because I wasn't connected to HERB; I was working with a Gatekeeper. I had to work hard to convince the Gatekeeper that my training programs were right for their organization. Did I get the sale? Yes, but it took much longer and required jumping a lot more hurdles than it should have."

This is the difference between going from the top down and going from the bottom up. It takes time to connect at the top, but once you're there it's a lot faster to get the sale done and a relationship secured.

Does this work 100 percent of the time? No. Nothing does. Eighty percent of salespeople are afraid to do the hard stuff. It's up to you to embrace these practices, make them your own, and put them to use.

We're asking you to do things that you might not be currently doing. The unknown can be frightening at times. However, we have given you the guidebook on how to do it, so forget about all the reasons it might not work and open your eyes to the possible positive outcomes instead.

We leave you with one more challenge to consider in order to help you create these new habits we have introduced in our book. If you think about all the information we provided, there is really nothing new that you did not already know. However, we did give you a deeper understanding and the competitive know-how to gain those all-important initial appointments you have to have to gain a customer. You are now a Competitive Seller when gaining first appointments! That is a huge achievement!

So now let's put your feet to the fire. Our challenge to you is to call us! Yes, you read that correctly. We are asking you to pick up the phone and try to set an appointment with us. Reading how to do it is one thing; putting it into action is another. We would rather you mess up with us than try this with a true prospect who could be your number-one customer.

Our phone numbers are below. Call either one of us and either leave a voicemail as if we were a prospect, or if we answer, attempt to get an appointment. Either way, we will provide you feedback if you make the effort to call.

If you take us up on this offer and tell us where to email you, we will email you a *Competitive Selling* guidebook for easy access to our system just for trying! So, what do you have to lose? Nothing!

We look forward to hearing from you!

Stacia Skinner	and	Marisa Pensa
(847) 577-4115		(678) 574-6072

RESOURCES

RATIOS SHEET

KNOW YOUR NUMBERS!

MONDAY	TUESDAY	WEDNESDAY	THURSDAY	FRIDAY
New Dials	New Dials	New Dials	New Dials	New Dials
Contacts	Contacts	Contacts	Contacts	Contacts
First Appointments	First Appointments	First Appointments	First Appointments	First Appointments
Voicemail	Voicemail	Voicemail	Voicemail	Voicemail
Voicemail Return	Voicemail Return	Voicemail Return	Voicemail Return	Voicemail Return
Email	Email	Email	Email	Email
Email Response	Email Response	Email Response	Email Response	Email Response

ACKNOWLEDGMENTS WHEN HANDLING THE "NO"

TAKE THEIR GUARD DOWN, REPEAT, REASSURE, RESUME!

RESPONSE #1: "I'm not interested."

> **ACKNOWLEDGMENT:** *I understand. Some of my best customers weren't interested at first until they saw the benefits [your company name] could provide. That's why I would like to talk with you further . . .*

> **REDIRECT:** *I understand you're not interested, but before we get off the phone, I'm just curious . . . what are you currently doing regarding [product or service you're selling]?*

> [Their answer]

> *That is exactly why we should talk further . . .*

RESPONSE #2: "This is really a bad time. Could you call me at the end of the quarter?"

> **ACKNOWLEDGMENT:** *I completely understand. I would be happy to contact you at the end of the quarter. But before I get you off the phone, I'm just curious . . . what's happening between now and the end of the quarter?*

> [Their answer]

That is exactly why we should talk further . . .

[If they state that this is still not the right time . . .]

I understand. Why don't I contact you on [date in the future] and we can set an appointment at that time?

[When you call back use the technique of a warm and fuzzy call at a later date.]

RESPONSE #3: "We're all set with what we're currently doing."

ACKNOWLEDGMENT: *I can appreciate that. Other customers I work with have also been happy with their current [supplier/vendor]; however, we have found ways that we can enhance what they offer. That's why I would like to speak further . . .*

REDIRECT: *I'm just curious . . . may I ask what [company/supplier] you are currently working with?*

[Their answer]

That is exactly why we should talk further, so I can tell you how we can be a secondary resource.

RESPONSE #4: "We heard you are expensive."

ACKNOWLEDGMENT: *I can appreciate that. Some of our other customers thought the same thing until they saw the benefits* *of what we had to offer and how we could work with their budgets. That's why I would like to talk further . . .*

REDIRECT: *Before I get you off the phone, I'm just curious . . . how do you decide, other than price, which [products/services] you will use for your organization?*

[Their answer]

Well, that is exactly why we should talk further, so you can see how we can be an additional resource to what they [provide/offer]. How is . . . ?

RESPONSE #5: "Is there anything you can send or email me instead?"

ACKNOWLEDGMENT: *I would be happy to send you some information; however, I would still like the opportunity to talk with you further . . .*

REDIRECT: *I'll be happy to send you something, but to get an idea of the best information to send you, I'm just curious . . . what do you currently use regarding [a specific product or service] for your organization?*

[Their answer]

*That is exactly why we should talk more now, so I can tell you about how we could **enhance** what they currently offer . . .*

RESPONSE #6: "I'm heading into a meeting right now. Could you call me back?"

> **ACKNOWLEDGMENT:** *I understand that you're busy. The only reason I'm calling is to set an appointment with you. How is Tuesday at 2:00?*

SUMMARY OF PATTERNS FOR EASY REFERENCE

1. BASIC CALLING PATTERN

Good morning, John.

This is Stacia Skinner from Creative Training Solutions. I don't know how familiar you are with our company, but we provide customized training programs that have helped companies improve their bottom lines.

The reason for my call today, John, is I'd like to set an [phone] appointment with you to discuss what you're currently doing regarding your training initiatives and share some observations and trends we are seeing within your industry.

How is Tuesday at 2:00?

2. CANVASSING PATTERN

Good morning—Riley? (Riley nods or responds with a correction) My name is Marisa Pensa from Methods in Motion. I'm hoping you can help me.

I need to get this information to your vice president of sales [or whatever title you are targeting]. Can you make sure that person receives it?

Thank you so much. Can you provide me with the name you will be forwarding this to so I can follow up with them?

I really appreciate your help. You wouldn't happen to have [his/her] phone number or extension, would you?

3. THE FOLLOW-UP CALL—CANVASSING

Good morning, John. This is Stacia Skinner from Creative Training Solutions.

I don't know if you're familiar with our company, but we provide customized sales training for a wide range of industries. I stopped by your office on [date] and left some information with [name] in your reception area.

The reason I'm calling today is to ask for your help. I'm trying to find the person in charge of your sales training. I'm hoping you can give me some guidance as to who that would be.

4. ENGAGING OVER THE PHONE FOR INSIDE SALES

Hi John. This is Marisa Pensa with Methods in Motion.

I was pointed specifically in your direction and I'm not sure how familiar you are with us. We are an industry leader in hands-on inside sales training. You might be familiar with us from attending an event or one of our webinars. Just curious . . . does our name ring a bell?

The reason for my call is that we've been working with a lot of businesses that are very similar to yours, really helping them reduce the frustrations of _____ and _____.

[Now transition to questioning]

Today I would like to get a better feel for how your company handles those things and share some ideas about how we may be able to help. By the way . . .

5. UPSELLING EXISTING CLIENTS

Good morning, John. This is Stacia Skinner with Creative Training Solutions. How is your Friday going so far? By the way, thank you again for your trust in us and for giving us your business. We really do appreciate it!

The reason for my call today is I was looking at your account and realized there are some opportunities you're not taking advantage of that I think would really make sense for your business. I'd like to set an appointment with you to discuss this in further detail. How does your schedule look for Tuesday at 2:00?

6. REACTIVATING DORMANT ACCOUNTS

Hi John. This is Marisa Pensa with Methods in Motion. [If you are new, state that you are new to the account]. The reason for my call is I was looking at your account and realized we haven't heard from you in some time. I'm just curious . . . did we do something wrong?

[If they say no]

Okay. Well, I would certainly like the opportunity to talk with you about some of the new things we are doing at Methods in Motion, and I'd like to set an appointment to discuss them with you in further detail. How does your schedule look on Tuesday at 2:00?

[If they say yes]

I'm so sorry to hear that! I would like the opportunity to discuss this in further detail and show you how we have changed. How does your schedule look on Tuesday at 2:00?

7. FOLLOW-UP WHEN YOU WERE ASKED TO CALL AT A LATER DATE

Hi John. This is Stacia Skinner with Creative Training Solutions. We provide customized training programs that have impacted many companies' bottom lines. The last time we spoke on [date], you and I agreed I would contact you today to set an appointment. How does your schedule look for Tuesday at 2:00?

8. CONNECTING WITH THE GRAND POOBAH

Good morning, Grand Poobah. This is Marisa Pensa with Methods in Motion. I'm hoping you can help me. I'm trying to find the person in charge of your sales training, and I really have nowhere else to turn. I'm hoping you can give me some guidance as to who that would be.

9. SAY HELLO TO SAM, HERB'S ASSISTANT

SAM: *HERB's office. This is Sam. How can I help you?*

YOU: *Oh, Sam, I'm really hoping you can! This is Stacia Skinner from Creative Training Solutions. I'm trying to reach HERB. [Or I've been trying to reach HERB for a while.] Do you know the best way for me to contact [him/her]?*

Or:

Sam, I'm really hoping you can! This is Marisa Pensa from Methods in Motion. We provide sales training, and I'm trying to reach HERB. Can you guide me as to the best way I can get a hold of [him/her]?

Or:

Sam, I'm really hoping you can. This is Stacia Skinner from Creative Training Solutions. We provide sales training, and I've been trying to reach HERB. By any chance do you hold [his/her] calendar?

Or:

Sam, I'm really hoping you can. This is Marisa Pensa from Methods in Motion. We provide sales training, and I am looking for the person who would be in charge of either your sales teams or training for your company. I am hoping you can provide me with some guidance since I have nowhere else to turn.

SAMPLE EMAILS AND HANDWRITTEN NOTES

FOLLOW-UP DOCUMENTS

1. Email—Confirm Initial Discussion
2. Thank-You Note—After Initial Appointment
3. Email—Confirm Site Visit
4. Email Thank-You Note—After Site Visit
5. Email—"Did we do something wrong?"
6. Email—"Tried unsuccessfully to reach you"
7. Thank-You Note—New Customer
8. Email—Secondary Resource

1. Email—Confirm Initial Discussion

Subject: Confirmation

Dear [prospect name],

It was a pleasure speaking with you today. I look forward to meeting you on [date and time] to explore how [your company name] can benefit your organization.

Please call if I can be of any help between now and our scheduled appointment. In the meantime, take a look at our information-filled website at [your web address].

Best regards,
[Signature]

2. Thank-You Note—After Initial Appointment

(Note is handwritten.)

Dear [prospect name],

Thank you for your time today. It was a pleasure meeting you. I appreciate the information you provided regarding your organization's [whatever it is you sell]. I believe we can be a great resource for you. I am confident we will be able to [mention something from the meeting]. Thank you again.

Best regards,
[Signature]

3. Email—Confirm Site Visit

Subject: Visit Confirmation

Dear [prospect name],

Thank you for agreeing to discover more about how [your company name] can positively affect your organization's [whatever it is you sell]. We look forward to having you experience our [what you offer] personally on [date and time].

Please forward this email to any others you would like to have join us for the site visit. We recommend that anyone with a strong influence on the decision be present for this visit. During our time together we will highlight the [name something they mentioned specifically] you had questions about.

Thank you again and we look forward to having you join us!

Best regards,
[Signature]

4. Email Thank-You Note—After Site Visit

Subject: Thank You

Dear [prospect name],

Thank you for your time and consideration. I hope you enjoyed your visit as much as we enjoyed having you. I am working on putting together the details of the options we discussed.

You did mention [something stated during the visit] and we are able to [what you plan to do].

I look forward to [seeing you/speaking with you] again on [date and time]. Thank you again for your time and interest in [your company name].

Best regards,
[Signature]

5. Email—"Did we do something wrong?"

Subject: Thank You

Dear [prospect name],

I know you expressed interest in [your company name] and I believe we stopped short of working together. I wanted to make sure we didn't do something wrong that is preventing us from doing business together.

I welcome the opportunity to reintroduce you to [your company name]. I will contact you on Tuesday afternoon to set an appointment to find out what it will take to earn your business.

Thank you and I look forward to speaking with you!

Best regards,
[Signature]

6. Email—"Tried unsuccessfully to reach you"

Subject: Tried Unsuccessfully to Reach [or Contact] You

Dear [prospect name],

In recent days I have tried to reach you by phone and thought email might be an easier way for us to connect.

My intention for reaching out is to schedule an appointment with you. I would like to share some observations and trends we have seen in your industry and how we have helped provide a positive impact on the bottom line.

How does your schedule look for us to get together at one of the times below?

Option 1: [Date/time]

Option 2: [Date/time]

Option 3: [Date/time]

If these are not convenient, please let me know if there are a couple other alternative dates that would be better for your schedule.

Thank you.

[Signature]

7. Thank-You Note—New Customer

(Note is handwritten)

Dear [name],

I want to personally take this opportunity to thank you for becoming a customer of [your company name]!

We're excited about working with you and helping you become the very newest success story at [your company name].

We work as a team and we are here to serve you, so please don't hesitate to contact us should you have any questions at all. We will be in touch.

Best regards,
[Signature]

8. Email—Secondary Resource

Subject: Thank you for the opportunity

Dear [prospect name],

It was a pleasure speaking with you today. From our conversation I know you are committed to [reason why your company is not an option right now].

Our mission is to make sure everyone has a positive experience with [your company name] and we would appreciate your keeping us in mind as a secondary resource in the future.

Thank you again for the opportunity to show you what we have to offer. I wish you much success.

All the best,
[Signature]

THE COMPETITIVE SELLING TRAINING SERIES: CUSTOMIZED FOR YOU!

GAINING THE FIRST APPOINTMENT:
Provides strategies and a process for gaining a first appointment with the right person.

OPPORTUNITY MANAGEMENT:
Provides a common language throughout the sales environment in order to gain continuous growth in an individual's sales pipeline.

BUILDING POWERFUL CONVERSATIONS:
Enhances the skill sets of sales representatives from hello to close and provides guidelines for gaining depth in the sales conversation.

BUILDING POWERFUL CONVERSATIONS FOR INSIDE SALES:
Introduces a sales process designed specifically for inside sales professionals who sell 100% over the phone, from start to finish, for both inbound and outbound call centers.

NETWORKING FOR SUCCESS:
Provides tips, strategies, and guidelines for representatives to gain the most from a networking event and trade show.

MAJOR ACCOUNT NAVIGATION:
The main focus is to provide a guideline when selling to multiple decision makers within an account. This program helps them find business in new and/or existing accounts in a complex sales environment.

THE EDGE SALES SIMULATION:
This program is like no other. It brings real-world chaos and pressure into a risk-free practice zone to increase sales performance and strategy.

ABOUT THE AUTHORS

STACIA SKINNER
PRESIDENT OF CREATIVE TRAINING SOLUTIONS,
LTD. (CTS) IN EASTON, MARYLAND

This is a second publication for Stacia as a well-known trainer and consultant. Her first book, *Sell Now,* was published in 2011 by Adams Media. Stacia launched her company in 2003 after being in the training industry for eight years. She brings more than twenty years of extensive sales training and thirty years of personal sales experience to her teachings. Prior to launching Creative Training Solutions, Ltd., Stacia worked in a variety of industries including specialty advertising, manufacturing, environmental, publishing, corporate travel, and meeting planning.

While working with a multitude of industries and helping thousands of salespeople throughout the years both domestically and internationally, passion, commitment, and gaining an understanding of her customers is what drives her success. Being able to help people excel in their careers of sales and seeing the returns from their success is what keeps her going to do more.

Stacia practices what she preaches by balancing the work of managing the company, going after new business, and developing and conducting trainings and keynotes. She brings a very upbeat, passionate, and enthusiastic style to all that she does!

MARISA PENSA
PRESIDENT OF METHODS IN MOTION IN ATLANTA, GEORGIA

Marisa launched Methods in Motion in 2004. Prior to that she held positions that included sales director with a major hotel chain and regional sales manager with a national telecommunications company.

Over the last fifteen years Methods in Motion has helped hundreds of companies from diverse industries grow their businesses, from office products / facilities maintenance to floor covering, technology/software, and equipment and safety products. Marisa knows that in life it's all about building good relationships.

Marisa has conducted sales training workshops throughout the U.S. and abroad, is certified by the Leadership Strategies Institute as an "Effective Facilitator," and is regularly published in *Independent Dealer Magazine.* Marisa lives out what she teaches every day and has a passion for helping sales teams improve their confidence and their enthusiasm for sales.

For more information:

Stacia Skinner
Creative Training Solutions, Ltd.
(847) 577-4115 (office)
stacia@cts-solutions.net
www.competitiveselling.net

Marisa Pensa
Methods in Motion
(678) 574-6072 (office)
marisa@methodsnmotion.com
www.competitiveselling.net

CPSIA information can be obtained
at www.ICGtesting.com
Printed in the USA
FSHW010618311019
63545FS